A View With a Room

By Kevin McDonough

A View With a Room

Copyright 2015 Kevin McDonough

This book is available in print at most online retailers and is licensed for your personal enjoyment only. This e-book may not be re-sold or given away to other people. If you would like to share this book with another person, please purchase an additional copy for each recipient.

If you're reading this book and did not purchase it, or it was not purchased for your use only, then please return to your favorite e-book retailer and purchase your own copy. Thank you for respecting the hard work of this author.

Copyediting by EbookEditingServices.com
Formatting by IRONHORSE Formatting
Book Design by P&N Graphics
Cover Art by Marie de Rémur

ISBN-13: 978-1502354372

Table of Contents

Somewhere Over the North Pole	3
Me, the Unwelcome Guest	9
The Hôtel Poubelle	15
Crêpe Grand Marnier	21
School's in Session	27
The Customer is Always Wrong	35
A Nuit Blanche	45
Dumped at the Concorde	50
Some Friendly Advice	53
Sunday with the Boss	56
Late, Right on Time	58
Snails & Dominique	63
Momma, The Door Nazi	75
Ghost Stories in Normandy	81
Costume Party	85
Riding the Rails	89
Two Gentlemen From Verona	93
Silvia, Rita, and a Flat Tire	98

Scheiße!	107
The Brothers of San Remo	111
Friend!	115
Goats in Trees, I Swear	120
A Night at the Opera	132
When Bobby Came to Visit	136
On Top of Samaritaine	144
Jane, a Balloon, and Marvin	147
It's Over	159
Updates	165
About the Author	167
A Sneak Peek of my next book, "Re-entry."	168

This is not a guidebook about Paris. Nor is it a how-to, fish-out-of-water, or (yawn), *The-French-Are-Different-Than-Us* book. There are plenty of those already, good and awful.

But, if you ever wondered what might happen if you dropped everything and moved to Paris and let come-what-may guide you, this book is for you. I can't promise everything that happened to me will happen to you. I can only hope.

I dedicate this book to my family, and the friends I met in this book. Without them, this book would not have been possible. And lastly, this book is for anyone who thought about doing what I did, but hasn't done it.

Yet.

Somewhere Over the North Pole

"You're *what?*" The man in the seat next to me squinted in disbelief, his brow furrowed deep enough to plant crops. I closed my book and looked out the airplane's window into darkness. There was no avoiding him on this eleven hour flight. He grabbed a handful of peanut bags and a soda from the cart. Our aisle was next to be served, but he couldn't wait.

"Why in the world do you want to go to Paris?" he demanded. I thought about informing him that he, too, was going to Paris, but he beat me to it. "I'm only connecting there to go to Frankfurt."

I'd had this discussion many times back home, but naively thought once I stepped on the plane I'd be finished with it. The airline's ticketing system had placed him next to me without a thought as to how we might get along. We were horrible traveling partners and could barely stand each other.

His hostility was pushed along by his endless supply of vodka mini-bottles he kept downing. And we were still climbing out of Los Angeles.

"I hate the French," he said.

3

"You said that already. Ever met one?" I asked, knowing the answer.

"Nope."

"Ever been there?"

"Nope. After you land, then what?" he asked, a bit cocky.

I was going to tell him about the endless possibilities; cafés, museums, history, shopping for croissants and wine, and on and on. That would shut him up. But when I turned to light into him, nothing came out.

The truth was, I did not have the slightest idea what to do once I landed. I had been so busy planning and packing, that I never got around to thinking about what I'd actually do.

I had enrolled in a language school, but that seemed a formality, something to pass the time until I really got rolling. And now here I was with Mr. Too Many Questions, who just nailed me to the wall with the simplest one.

Two experiences shaped why I was doing this. First, working in television production, I saw the writing on the wall, and it spelled Reality TV. It oozed in when no one was looking, like an oil slick, then pounced with minuscule budgets fueling a low risk/high reward storm that flattened all but a few game shows and soap operas, and consolidated prime-time into a few select producers to churn out endless spin-offs. Cookie cutter production, we called it.

Secondly, I had been seeing a girl, at least I thought I was. Lately she had been a bit skittish about things. We all get skittish about things at one time or another. But this one skittered right out of my life.

Our Sunday morning ritual was the local coffee shop for breakfast and the Sunday *Times*. But one weekend she balked. She had things to do and wouldn't be able to share in the buttermilks and coffee.

So I headed out alone for a paper at the corner news stand. I was waiting for the light to change when the hair bristled on the back of my neck. In the passenger seat of a car that had stopped for the red light, there she was. She hid her face, but it was her. I could even tell what she was saying to the handsome stud behind the wheel. "Is he looking this way? Did he see me? I can't believe he's there. Go, go, go!" She peeked through her fingers and was so stunned to see me, all she could do was stare as I passed in front of her. I watched the taillights disappear around the corner. And her with it.

I may be off by a few dozen, but Los Angeles has around two hundred quadrillion people in it. What were the odds that we would meet on that corner when we shouldn't have? Hey, her fault for picking that street.

I read the paper at the counter and saw that the shows I was working on would not be picked up for another season. It didn't surprise me. Most of the staff was shocked we still had a job. I gave the entire paper to the guy next to me.

The pancakes were hot, smothered in syrup, and delicious. And just like that, my future came into focus, clear as the shock on her face when she saw me. I had been thrown two strikes, but I refused to let life throw a third one past me. I would miss my family and friends, but I wouldn't miss her. Maybe a little.

I had gotten the bug to make the leap across the Atlantic on my first trip a few years before. The moment I stepped off the shuttle near the Arc de Triomphe, I never wanted to leave. Since that moment, not a day passed that I didn't think of Paris. The idea of going back for an extended stay rattled in my head so loudly that after that first trip, I enrolled in a French language course.

It had always been fun, thinking about moving to Paris, but now to actually make the move seemed overwhelming. Could I really do it? I attacked the idea from the other side. I asked myself if I didn't go, would I always regret it? Of course I would. I'd beat myself up every day I woke up here and not there. I finished my pancakes and never looked back.

I went home and made a list of people who had made similar decisions to chuck it all and follow a dream. The only name I came up with was Homer Simpson, but he went to Clown College.

The only fly in the ointment so far was sitting next to me, now passed out with his empties rolling across his tray. That, and my wool coat. That one extravagant purchase was as big a pain as the guy next to me. Too bulky to pack, and no room in the overhead, I had to stuff it under my seat. And I kept stepping on it, scuffing it up.

At least I could gather my thoughts in silence. I made a to-do list. Number One, "Find Apartment." I had declined to check the box when I enrolled at the language school in Paris to have one waiting for me. No, I had to find a pied-à-terre on my terms.

Also, I'm cursed. I love to travel, but hate to fly. I don't like to think where the plane might go down, but the pilot kept reminding us; the Rocky Mountains, the Great Lakes, the jagged polar ice cap. But there we were, rocketing to the other side of the planet, barreling down on Paris, nose up, hopefully.

About an hour outside of Paris passengers started to stir, sensing we'd arrive soon. My hands were clammy. Why didn't anyone try to talk me out of it? Well, everyone did try to talk me out of it, and this is what happens when you don't listen to your friends.

I wore my wool coat in line for Immigration, sweating like a pig. It looked horrible after eleven hours crumpled under my seat. I just wanted to get through, get my bags, and escape to freedom.

The man in front of me grabbed his passport from the window and exited through the glass doors. I slid my things up to the window.

"Passport," the officer behind the glass droned.

"What?" I pressed my ear to the mouthpiece in the glass. "Again?"

A year of French classes and I couldn't understand the simplest demand. A woman behind me stepped up, I thought to help.

"He wants your passport, stupid. He's Immigration. What else would he want?" Then she handed me my passport. "Here, it fell out of that army blanket you're wearing."

"I had to stuff it under the seat," I said, defensively.

"You should have stuffed it down the toilet."

The officer studied my photo, then me, then slid it back. I was anxious for him to ask me something so I could redeem myself. "Passez."

"What?" I asked, ear stuck to the metal mouthpiece again.

The woman muscled past me to the window. "He wants you to go. That makes two of us. And get rid of that coat. You're in Paris, for chrissakes!"

I got my luggage and headed for the platform of the RER, the train that would whisk me into Paris. I took stock of my new life so far; a year of French lessons and unable to converse at the most elementary level, no plan other than an address of a friend of a friend who grudgingly agreed to let me sleep on her floor until I could get settled. So far so bad.

I hopped on the RER. As it pulled away, I listened to bits of conversation from the other passengers. I understood nothing, but it felt good to hear it. I tracked the stops on the map over the door: Sevran-Livry, Aulnay-Sous-Bois, Blanc-Mesnil, Le Bourget, counting them down to the Grand Central of Paris, Châtelet, then finally to Saint-Michel.

Out the right side of the train, through the haze, was what it was all about. The tip of the Eiffel Tower pierced the sky as we rumbled on. Really rolling now. The green hills of the suburbs gave way to industrial stacks and graffiti. My heart raced as I looked over my right shoulder. Sacré-Cœur, that majestic wedding cake of a church, floated into view from the top of the butte at Montmartre. It was the view from Sacré-Cœur that had given me the idea to return for a longer stay.

I stepped off at Saint-Michel and watched the RER's taillights disappear into the tunnel. It reminded me of that awful Sunday when my girl rode off with that guy. Already it seemed so long ago.

I surfaced at Place Saint-Michel and its fountain, one of my favorite places in Paris. Young kids sat around it, boys splashing girls and laughing, flirting really. Lovers watched them, remembering when they did the same. It was the perfect place for a rendezvous and I hoped I would have many.

I crossed the street and walked onto the Saint-Michel Bridge over the Seine. The scent of crêpes filled the air. I turned slowly taking it all in; upriver Nôtre Dame sat on the Île de la Cité, Sainte-Chapelle across the way, then downriver to the Pont Neuf and Vert Galant on the tip of the Île. Everywhere people were strolling, talking, darting through beautiful traffic jams. I'm in Paris!

Me, the Unwelcome Guest

I pulled out the address of the friend of a friend. I knew roughly where it was, but I'd have to hump it. I slung my overnight bag over my shoulder, picked up my suitcases, and headed out. I cut through the Latin Quarter, always good to see that, but in two blocks I was sweating like a pig. My wool coat would work wonders in winter, but it was late spring, warm, and there was no place to carry it except on me.

I sat on a suitcase and took a breather. There was no way to hail a cab, and my wallet was buried in my coat somewhere. Nothing to do but forge ahead on foot.

After several turns onto small streets, I was still looking for number 36. I saw 12 above a small store and figured it couldn't be much farther. After two long blocks I was at 14. I had to rest again.

When I finally arrived, the friend of a friend opened her door. She was marginally welcoming, and I couldn't blame her. Who wants a sweaty stranger knocking on their door for a place to crash? We exchanged niceties and she pointed to a corner of her very small apartment.

She offered me water over a stilted conversation about our mutual friend, who had come up with this less than ideal suggestion for me to stay there. It was almost dinnertime, so I offered to take her to dinner.

After a few glasses of red wine, she realized I wasn't that bad. I think. I had given her a bad impression wearing my scuffed-up coat and showing up with a year's worth of luggage. It was such a relief to finally be in Paris, I probably ran my mouth a bit too much.

She sipped her wine and listened to my plan of spending a year in Paris. I had a million questions to ask. She had only one. "When are you leaving?"

****

It was the most uncomfortable night of my life. And not because of the hardwood floor I slept on, that was a breeze compared to the walk home. I struggled to think of interesting things to say, but after the long flight, it was impossible. It was painfully obvious she didn't want me staying. This whole idea had rotted like fruit in the hot sun.

Jet lag and aching muscles be damned, I awoke pre-dawn, wrote a thank-you note, and slipped out into the dark. I walked five blocks before I realized I had no idea where to go. The only place I came up with was the language school. It was too early, so I grabbed a sidewalk table on Rue Saint-André-des-Arts and ordered coffee and a croissant. Then another coffee and croissant. Then another. No better way to kill time, but then it was time to move on.

I entered the small passageway to the school and walked around a cluster of nervous students, puffing their lungs out at the entrance. Some things never change.

The lobby was packed with kids half my age scurrying about with books and cigarettes in hand. On a wall was a bulletin board with some 3x5 index cards. It was slim pickings, but I copied down some addresses and headed out. Out I went. With a piece of paper and fifty pounds of luggage. Available cabs are as rare as in midtown Manhattan, but at this hour I found one. I handed the driver the paper and off we went.

We screeched up to a nondescript apartment building. I got out and walked up to a heavy metal gate with an intercom embedded in the concrete wall next to it. It had one button on it, so I pressed it.

A woman's voice squawked through the tinny speaker, "Oui?" Terrifying.

"Uh, apartment?"

An explosion of French boomed out, then: BUZZ.

The security gate popped open and I entered. I humped my luggage to the fourth floor making a mental note of no elevator. Madame and Monsieur opened the door and stared at me as if I were a Martian. They led me into their salon. It looked like Norman Bates lived there, but without the charm.

Their frosty demeanor sucked the life out of the room. They alternated reciting a litany of rules and regulations that I simply must adhere to. At least I thought that's what they were saying. I had no intention of renting the room, so just for ducks I asked where it was. Madame pointed to the sofa. There was no room, it was a sofa for rent. I pointed at it in disbelief.

"That?" Yes, that, and breakfast was between seven and eight, dinner at seven. No lunch. No exceptions. I'm sure most eighteen-year olds would jump at the chance to sleep on a Parisian sofa. But my back and patience wasn't what it used to be, and I was wiser than an eighteen-year old. Not wise enough to check the box on the application form for the school to handle my housing, but still.

Madame and Monsieur were shocked when I let myself out with my luggage. They weren't used to rejection. Paris sells itself. But not today.

Another place offered a bedroom/storage room combo I'd have to share with Maurice the hamster. I didn't even bother with the third. The driver told me it was in the *banlieu*, and I didn't come to Paris to live in the suburb. I decided to throw myself at the mercy of the language school.

I dropped my luggage in front of the receptionist. "Ooh, looks like somebody forgot to check that box on the application form." Her English was as good as it was obnoxious.

I looked pathetic, sweating like a pig in May. She pulled a stack of 3x5 cards from a drawer, and shuffled through them like a Vegas dealer. She came up with three, tossed one aside and studied the other two. "You want a busy quartier or a quiet one?"

"Quiet. I'll visit the busy ones."

She dialed a number and handed me the receiver. The only thing worse than speaking to French strangers, is speaking to French strangers on the phone. You can't read their lips. A woman's no-nonsense voice in English was on the other end.

"I have an apartment in the 15th. I'll meet you there in an hour. Southeast corner." She hung up. I think her name was Laurie. The receptionist was curious.

"I'm meeting her in an hour. Thank you."

"Je vous en prie, monsieur. And no more English, it's not allowed during school hours."

"Got it. I mean, okay. Oui."

****

Laurie hooked her arm through mine as I exited the Métro and dragged me down the street. She moved quickly, with long, wavy, hippie hair, past what would become my patisserie, boulangerie, fromagerie, crêperie, pharmacie, charcouterie, and la poissonière. We whipped around a corner, up a slight hill, and buzzed our way into the breezeway of a building I never saw the outside of.

She waved to a plump, smiling woman in a doorway, who wiped her hands on her apron and waved to us. She would be my concièrge. She and Laurie exchanged quick pleasantries as we dashed across the grass of an inner courtyard and into the back building.

We stepped into a rickety elevator. Laurie slammed the collapsible iron gate and hit the 6th floor button. We bumped and rattled up the narrow shaft of the circular staircase. She rattled a skeleton key into a door and pushed it open. Scuffed-up wooden floors led down a short entryway. On the left was a shelf of tattered books. "Kitchen's on the right. Don't blink or you'll miss it."

She was right. The small table only had one chair. Another one would have blocked the oven door. The living room had a futon, armoire, and a TV. I opened the tall windows and looked down on the courtyard. A young couple passed by, arm in arm, and disappeared inside. "Vacuum cleaner and iron are in the closet. Notify the concierge when the butane tank gets low. You're not going to find anything better."

"Uh-huh," I mumbled, not listening.

I followed her into the bathroom. It was bigger than expected with a free-standing tub. Shelves were crammed with knick-knacks, trinkets, and souvenirs from her travels. Coiled around the tub faucet hung what seemed like fifty feet of metal hose with a showerhead on the end. I could probably water plants in the kitchen with it. Or the downstairs neighbor's.

At the far end she threw open a large window. I looked down at the rear of a boulangerie. Cars zoomed down a narrow street. Two men were arguing over a parking space, poking each other in the chest to ram their point home. "Look up, Dumbo."

I looked up. My breath caught in my throat. Across the city, past the tumbling maze of rooftops, perfect as a painting, stood the Eiffel Tower. I couldn't take my eyes off it. Laurie joined me at the window. We shared the view like old pals. "You're new here," she said. "You'll have some rough days. But you'll always come home to this."

I had seen the Tower many times before, from every angle: the steps of Sacré-Cœur, with a bottle of wine on the Vert Galant in the middle of the Seine, from Trocadèro, until the power company put it to sleep. But never from an apartment. "Three months in advance. Plus two months security."

"I'll take it," I said, still mesmerized.

"Of course you will. You can have it tomorrow if you bring the money." We shook hands on the deal and set a time to meet the next day. She turned quickly to leave, but not before I saw a tear in her eye.

The Hôtel Poubelle

I caught the receptionist before she left for the day.
"Ca va?" she asked. Everything okay?
I tried to explain I really could speak a little, but she probably heard that from every student who came through the doors. I asked her for one more favor. Could she recommend a place to stay for the night?
"La Poubelle." I'd heard that word before but, like every other word since I had landed, I couldn't place it. Worse, she was sticking to the no English mandate. "L'hôtel Poubelle est par là, à droite, première droite, et tout au fond. Voilà." And with that, she grabbed her coat and left. I grabbed my things and left. If she could do it, so could I.
I heard "droite," right, twice, so I turned right when I could and right again, into a dead-end alley. Was she pulling my leg? This had to be it, but it was creepy. A trash truck couldn't fit down here, which explained the odor. Then I remembered: "Poubelle." Trash can. The Trash Can Hotel. Boy, I can pick 'em.
Most of the ground floor spaces were boarded up. I was about to get out of there when faint Middle Eastern music lured me deeper. Before I knew it, I was standing

in front of a splintered door. A sputtering neon sign flashed: "Hôtel Poubelle." In the window was a cardboard sign scribbled in several languages: "Always Full But Always Room."

With nothing to lose but my life, I stepped inside. Snake charmer music swirled around me. Incense, and worse, or better, depending on your choice, hung in the air and stung my nose. Backpackers were sprawled on the floor, on the staircase, and in the doorway. Colored scarves hung over lamps splashing odd shades on the walls.

Holding court over this weird scene was Madame Renée, a large, imposing woman dressed in layers of black. She sat on a stack of pillows behind a desk piled with junk. Her jet-black hair cascaded down her shoulders in an organized mess. She puffed on a hand-rolled cigarette through a long holder, letting the smoke ooze out of her teeth.

She waved me over. I stepped over bodies and backpacks. She stared into my eyes as if trying to detect a character flaw. Satisfied, she spun around a spiral notebook. I signed in. She studied my signature, then my face. From under a pile of papers, she pulled out a skeleton key with a 6 on it and pointed up the rickety stairway.

The stairway was so rotted I had to test each step before putting my full weight on it. When I got to the landing, the room doors hung crooked on their hinges, leaving slanting gaps at the top and bottom. A room key was a formality. The latches didn't reach the doorjamb. I pushed open Room 6. There was a young couple having a terrific mid-day romp on the squeaky bed. I turned the key the other way. I was in Room 9.

Room 9 was all mine, and six others. Rucksacks were piled to the ceiling against two walls. I dragged my bags in, flopped onto what was probably a bed years ago. A spring coiled into my spine. I bent it away, rolled over, and fell asleep.

I didn't wake up until the next morning. I stumbled downstairs. The lobby was empty, everyone gone for the day. There was even a semblance of cleanliness to the place. Madame Renée poked her head out of the kitchen drying a dish.

"Bonjour, monsieur!" Madame Renée smiled sweetly at me. "Tu as bien dormi?" She wanted to know if I had slept well. I nodded, rubbing my face to wake up. "Ca va, monsieur?"

"Comme si, comme ça." I wiggled my hand to let her know it could have been better.

"Américain?" She wanted to keep the conversation going.

"Oui. Do you speak English?" I asked, squinting.

"Small English."

"Little English," I corrected.

She playfully slapped her forehead. Madame was actually shy. "I speak little English." She wanted to know what I was doing in Paris. I explained I had come to live in Paris for a year. I dug out the crumpled paper with my address. She nodded her approval of the area, then brought me coffee and a croissant.

After a well-needed shower and settling up the bill, she assured me I could call her for any reason. She hugged me. I shoved my luggage into a taxi she had called for me and we squeezed down the narrow alley.

At the apartment, Laurie was tossing some clothes into a pillowcase. She was moving in with her lover, but they didn't want to give this one up. She demonstrated the water heater, (mounted from the ceiling, upside down, in the kitchen), and butane tank for the stove.

The old buildings had thick cement walls, so jackhammering to plumb each apartment would have reduced the building to rubble. As a result, every stove gets a butane tank instead. Like camping out at home.

Yesterday Laurie lingered. Today she wanted out. She grabbed a few paperbacks off the hall shelf, then stepped into the elevator and rattled down. I went to the window and watched her cross the courtyard, her light footsteps tapping on the pavement. She turned. We waved, then she disappeared down the street.

It was dusk before I had any sense of rhythm to the place. I found a good station on the radio and began to move in. My new home didn't have much, but it had everything.

First thing, I wanted to hang my large Michelin map of Paris I'd bought at home. I had never opened it, and when I did, it was so big I had to drape it over furniture, fearing it would tear under its own weight.

I found some wall tacks and a small hammer in a junk drawer in the kitchen. It took an hour, but I got it up on the one large wall. It had everything on it, streets, train stations, bus and Métro lines, hospitals, pharmacies, parks, schools, churches, monuments, museums.

Next, I wanted to iron my clothes before putting them away. It gave me a sense of a new start in life. After the third shirt, it hit me. Why was I ironing my clothes on my first night in Paris? My back was killing me. It had been a long day. I walked into the bathroom and looked at the cast iron tub and box of bubble bath on the shelf. Why not? I hadn't had a bubble bath since I was five.

I ran the tub and poured in the bath powder. As it filled with bubbles, clusters floated to the ceiling. I opened the steamed-up window. The Eiffel Tower was framed perfectly, glowing amber against the dark sky. I turned the light off and lit a candle. I felt my way into the tub and sank to my chin into a warm ocean of bubbles.

I closed my eyes. Images flashed through my brain; the plane ride over, Saint-Michel, "When are you leaving?" the receptionist at the language school, Laurie, my new apartment. I felt a great weight lifted from my shoulders.

Somehow I had done it. Years of thinking, worrying, and planning had come to this. I had done everything I set out to do. Except eat.

Bathing is not as basic an instinct as hunger. I tried to ignore the pangs, but they kept coming. No matter how hard I shut my eyes, my stomach bucked and shook like an old jalopy. I had to eat.

I pulled the plug and watched the bubbles swirl down the drain, except the millions that clung to me. I stood up and looked in the mirror. I looked like a molting snow angel.

Without thinking I twisted the faucet handle. The metal hose uncoiled with a jerk. Freezing water exploded out of the showerhead as it shot up like a bottle rocket. It spun in the air, spraying water everywhere, extinguishing the candle.

It dove at me like a striking cobra, slammed into the tub and rattled like a caged animal. I groped in the dark but it rammed my chest, knocking the wind out of me.

It slithered along the bottom, then launched up the side of the tub like an alpine jumper. It ricocheted off the ceiling, chipped a wall tile, and sprayed the room like an indoor car wash.

I grabbed the metal hose, but not before it whacked a shelf of knick-knacks across the room. It was a possessed Water Wiggle. It squirmed away from me and knocked the clock off the wall.

I belly-flopped on it and tuck-and-rolled. I groped for the faucet handle and shut the water off. It fought to the end, but finally died a slow death.

The room was soaked. The towels drenched, the clock shattered. The candle floated by. How did this happen? A minute ago I was soaking in warm bubbles staring at the Tower. Now this.

I coiled the snake around the faucet and climbed out. I looked in the dripping mirror. Well, I thought, that's one way to get rinse the bubbles off. I squeezed the wet towels out the window and used one to push the debris into a corner.

I went to the kitchen and dried off with some cocktail napkins I found in a drawer. I opened the small refrigerator. It was as empty as my stomach. It was after 8:00pm. The markets would be closed. Nothing to do but hit the streets and find something.

Crêpe Grand Marnier

I dressed and locked up my apartment. I found a shortcut through a sloping park to Rue de Vaugirard. Restaurants were open, but I didn't feel like dining alone. Then I smelled crêpes. A jovial man at a sidewalk crêpe stand was ladling hot plates with batter. Judging from the line snaking down the sidewalk there were others with empty fridges too.

I got in line but was too far away to read the menu. I studied every crêpe as it passed by; Nutella, fruit preserves, ham and cheese. As the line inched closer I saw what I wanted. Crêpe Grand Marnier. I could picture it in my head; a hot crêpe drizzled with orange liqueur, sprinkled with sugar and rolled in a napkin. A little sweet, a little tart, and maybe a little buzz. And then it was my turn.

"Monsieur, vous désirez?" the jovial man asked me, as he ladled batter onto the hot griddle. "Monsieur?"

My right arm shot out, index finger pointing skyward. I opened my mouth to speak, but a woman in a red dress passed by. The street went silent as she stepped between two parked cars and gracefully jaywalked. Cars skidded to a stop. She glided to the other sidewalk where she gained another set of admirers as she disappeared around a corner.

"Monsieur." He wasn't so jovial as he tossed the charred crêpe into the trash. "Vous désirez!" I blinked back to reality and gave it my best shot, still pointing skyward.

"Crêpe Grarn...Marn yarn yer ray." My throat seized up. I couldn't do the guttural "r" so I growled it like a true American.

"Pardon?" Just my luck, first night out and I get a guy who doesn't understand the language. I ran it all together to hide my inability to speak.

"Crêpe Grarn Marnyarnyerray." I sounded like a garbage disposal.

The Crêpe Man blinked, horrified. The ladle dangled from his hand, dribbling batter onto the sizzling plate.

A man behind me burst out laughing. Worse, the young woman with him was laughing louder. She leaned against the café glass for support, holding her sides. Laughter, like the plague, is contagious. My gaffe shot through the crowd like lightning. I didn't bother with him, he was already on his knees, helpless, so I focused on her. She doubled over, laughing so hard she looked like a pretzel. I waited (what else could I do, standing on a corner in Paris, famished?).

"Finished?" I snapped.

She tried three times to speak, but each time she crumpled into fits of laughter. Gasping for air, she dabbed her smeared mascara and spoke in that beautiful clipped French accent. "Say it again, please."

"I said, are you finished?" Oh, you should have *seen* how indignant I was! Hands on hips, jaw and eyes set. She couldn't have cared less.

"No, before. What kind of crêpe?" she asked, already biting her lip to stifle another round of hysteria.

The crowd edged closer, in case I stupidly took the bait. Which I stupidly did. My nose was so far out of joint I looked like a Picasso. But I would defy this young woman at all costs.

"Crêpe..." I began, "Grarn...Marn...yeranyeryay. What of it?" Down she went in another fit of laughter. She had to hang onto her friend to not fall down. And he was no better, relaying every humiliating syllable to the curious crowd. The young woman staggered up to the Crêpe Man, still catching her breath and dabbing her eyes.

"Monsieur, mon nouvel ami aimerait bien une crêpe Grand Marnier." The Crêpe Man ladled batter onto his hot skillets.

"Oui, mademoiselle. Tout de suite!" I think he was glad to finally understand somebody.

Nouvel ami? *New friend?*

"Et deux crêpes au chocolat pour nous." Two chocolate crêpes for her and her friend.

"D'accord, mademoiselle! Deux crêpes au chocolat!" He hopped right to it. I couldn't believe it. He understood her perfectly, but not me.

The young woman turned to me and extended her hand. "Framboise."

"Your name is Raspberry?" I asked. A nickname, she told me. She introduced her friend, Mikel. We all shook hands, and they waited.

"Do you have a name?" Framboise asked.

"Are you going to laugh?" I asked, my nose still out of joint.

"Probably," she replied, ready to burst. She wanted me to choke on another "r." Thank goodness my name wasn't Rory; we'd have to call an ambulance. We stepped out of line. My jets were cooling down, so I thanked her for ordering. "We go to café. You come?" she asked. Mikel handed Framboise her chocolate crêpe. He held mine back.

"Say it again," Mikel said. "Please, for me." I knew I could do it if I just relaxed. Mikel's eyes widened in anticipation as I gathered my nerve.

Everyone was still watching, even Crêpe Man. All I had to do was say "Crêpe Grand Marnier" and be done with it. It seemed so simple, so why not get it over with and have some fun? "Crêpe..." I began.

"Forget crêpe," Mikel said. "What kind?"

"Grarn...Marn...yeranyeryay."

An intense year in language school and that's what came out. Framboise and Mikel hung on the crêpe stand, crying in laughter. Stubborn Irish, I suppose, but I kept at it, regressing each time until I couldn't even get "Crêpe" out. I gave up. I got a few supportive pats on the back as the line moved forward, but it was, and still is, one of the most humiliating nights of my life.

And that's how I met my first friend in Paris.

****

Thirty minutes later we were sitting at a sidewalk café in the shadow of Église Saint-Germain, and down the street from the legendary cafés Deux Magots and Café de Fiore. Mikel and Framboise were good friends, out for the night. They grew up around the corner from each other in the 7th arrondissement, walking distance to the Rodin Museum, Eiffel Tower, and the Seine.

We talked like old friends, but mostly we laughed and laughed and laughed. She asked me, Crêpe Grand Marnier aside, how was my first night in my apartment? I touched the rising bump on the back of my head where the metal snake got a lucky shot in, but only shrugged.

They couldn't understand why I left the sunshine, palm trees, and blue Pacific of California, to come to Paris. I couldn't fathom they weren't staring at the Eiffel Tower. Ah, they scoffed, they see it all the time.

I couldn't have asked for a better first night, but it was late. The Métro was closed so they offered to drive me home, but I didn't know where I lived. I followed Laurie the first time, and then I walked it from memory, but didn't know the address.

Framboise found a map under the seat, but it was hopeless. I suggested we tail bus #49. Better yet, if we could find it, we could drive up that sloping park I had cut through on the way down, an idea I attribute to the wine. Framboise kept studying the map. The French don't waste time debating what you say, they just pretend you never said it. Which I like. But we found it.

We couldn't exchange phone numbers because I didn't know mine. I would call them. I rode the elevator to the sixth floor, fiddled with the lock, aimed my weary body toward the sofa, and was asleep before my head hit the pillow.

****

The knocking was relentless. A slow, constant tap-tap-tap. "Monsieur?" Tap-tap-tap. I stumbled across the room and opened the door.

"Bonjour, monsieur!" It was the concièrge. I recognized her when I had passed through the breezeway with Laurie. She was past me and into the kitchen before I caught up with her.

Her thick eyeglasses magnified her eyes like they were underwater. She was cheerful as a sunny day, and talked non-stop. I understood none of it.

She asked me questions. I answered what I think she asked, but she didn't know what I was talking about. That made two of us. We finally settled into a rhythm of nods and an occasional "Ah, oui?" and it seemed to work.

Then she pulled some documents from her blouse. Laurie had warned me about French paperwork. "Reams of ramblings" she called it. I had no idea what I was signing, I just scribbled where she pointed. There's something about signing your life away that brings everything into focus. I realized I was standing there in my skivvies. It was too late to run, so I stood there and dug sleep out of my eyes as she spoke. Suddenly, silence. She squinted through her thick glasses waiting for an answer.

"Uh, n-non," I stammered, with a finger stuck in my eye. She kept staring. "I mean, oui."

That was the ticket. She smiled and stuffed the contracts down her blouse. I guess that's where concièrges keep important documents. She tapped the butane tank beside the stove, listened, then twisted its valve open. Gas hissed through the line. She opened the oven door, then started looking for matches.

In my limited experience lighting ovens, she had the order wrong, but what was I going to say standing in my underwear? She went through her pockets, then my cabinets and drawers. My skin went cold listening to the hissing gas.

She pulled a drawer out too far and spilled silverware on to the floor, sifted through its contents on her hands and knees, and unfortunately came up with a match.

She struck it. I froze. It's true, your entire life passes before you in a flash. And when it did, I'd forgotten how much fun I'd had. But it looked like it was all coming to a sad end in my tiny kitchen in Paris. She lit the pilot light.

Whoosh! The oven roared to life. Unfazed, she climbed to her feet, flicked a few charred eyebrow hairs away, and lit all four burners. Everything seemed to be working perfectly. She pointed at the tank and explained who knows what, then shut it all down.

And just like that, with a firm handshake and a smile, she was gone.

School's in Session

Monday morning. First day of school. I rode the Métro, staring at the sad, bored faces across from me. They were slumped in their seats, beaten down with the tedium of commuting. They shuffled on and off, and plopped down with heavy sighs. How could anyone be so down living in Paris?

I changed at Sèvres-Babylone and got off at Odéon. I love the 6th arrondissement. It has everything: churches, cafés, quiet narrow streets, and movie houses. I passed sidewalk cafés filled with people talking over coffee and croissants. I envied them, but I was going to my oral placement exam. Based on my Crêpe Grand Marnier debacle, I pretty much knew the outcome, so I ducked into a bar and ordered a glass of Côtes du Rhône. The bartender studied me as I gulped it a little too quickly for the early hour.

"Ca va, monsieur?" he asked with genuine interest, wanting to know if I was all right. I pointed down the street to the school.

"Examen orale." He understood immediately and splashed a little extra into my glass. No charge.

"Bonne chance, monsieur." Good luck. And I'd need it.

I pushed past a horde of kids nervously smoking and entered the school. There was another mob at the front desk, hurling questions at the receptionist. I threw my arms up, in the unspoken question, "Where do I go?" She pointed to a door. I opened it, tripped over a mop and stepped in a bucket. Broom closet.

I couldn't get the damn thing off me, no matter how hard I kicked. A tiny woman, with a lion's mane of wavy hair, assessed the situation, hands on hips. She knelt down and pried the handle back. I stepped out. She was gone before I could thank her.

Upstairs, students paced the hallway mumbling verb conjugations, and mentally cramming for the exam. A young girl staggered out of a room, glassy eyed, and bumped into me. A stern and very pregnant woman leaned out and hollered my name. I followed her in and sat down. She cross-checked my name on the master sheet.

"Bonjour" she said, business like.

"Bonjour" I squeaked, my face flushed from the wine. She made a check mark on a sheet.

"Vous parlez français depuis longtemps?" She wanted to know if I'd been speaking French long. *Not long enough, apparently*. Another check. "Vous ne comprenez rien du tout?" I recognized the words, I just couldn't make any sense out of them. I squirmed in my seat. Another check. She studied me closely, like a prison guard deciding on my parole, then scribbled a note.

"Pourquoi êtes-vous venu à Paris?" Why did I come to Paris? My arm shot up again, finger pointing skyward, but my brain was blank. She made a final note.

"Merci" she said, and pointed to the door.

I was assigned to Room 12. That must be where they store the dunce caps. The tables were in a square U, forcing us to face each other. The pregnant woman entered and wrote "Odette" on the board. She ripped into blistering French while the others listened, nodded, and casually jotted notes. If they were dunces, they were the smartest dunces I'd ever seen. Then my nightmare started. Introductions.

There was Alessandra and Silvia from Italy, Olga and Isobel from Mexico, Yoko from Japan, Juan from Spain, Molly, the only other American, Dae Song from Korea, Sandra from Switzerland, Bÿke from Belgium.

And then there was Markus from Switzerland, the land of storybook beauty and Alpine majesty, its people groomed to perfection. Except Markus, who had the hygiene of a sloth. His jagged-nailed, tobacco-stained fingers and teeth were encrusted with what looked like tar. His hair had an oily sheen, his skin a dull patina, like oxidized paint. His shirts were wrinkled, half-tucked, and on this first day of class, inside out. His belt missed loops, cinching his pants into an unsightly bulge up front. He looked like an unmade bed.

He answered everything with an enthusiastic "Yes-yes!" and had such a wide-eyed innocence and winning personality, we all wanted to be around him. Just not too close. How he got that way in only eighteen years is anyone's guess.

Everyone was grammatically and linguistically ahead of me. They made mistakes, but nothing close to my crêpe disaster with Framboise.

Odette was a verbal hurricane. She seemed to be paid by the word. She would initiate a topic and everyone would jump in. I had a death grip on the table, afraid if I let go I'd fly out the window.

Back home, my French classes met once a week. But this was four hours a day, five days a week. More if you wanted it, with afternoon classes, and a language and video lab. It was a staggering amount of information to absorb, or in my case, repel.

I sat in constant fear of being called upon, which made the classes tense and slow, but somehow the days passed quickly. I soon got into a rhythm; wake up, eat, hop on the Métro, hop off, rush to school, flop into my seat and think, why?

Then bolt after the last class, rush to the Métro, grab dinner, and go home. By the end of the first week I could barely get out of bed. I don't know about you, but I'm not as young as I used to be.

At the end of the first week I was staring into the hall envying the janitor who didn't worry about being called on, when Odette asked me, "Monsieur, vous avez un appartement?" I caught "appartement" and I sensed a trap. Everyone was staring at me with anticipation.

"Uh...oui," I said.

The class exploded in cheers. You could feel the pressure escape like a leaky tire. They jumped up slapping high fives and cheering. One girl actually touched Markus. "Yes-yes-yes!" Wow, three.

They were all in their late teens to early twenties, still under the thumb of their parents who were paying for their summer romp--I mean, cultural exchange--in Paris. The deal in that bargain was they had to live with a host family, not unlike Madame and Monsieur, who offered me their sofa for a king's ransom.

Host families ruled the roost. Breakfast was at 7:00am. If you overslept, tough. Dinner at 6:00pm. If you were late, tough. It might sound trivial, but in Paris it creates a problem. Classes ran until 1:00pm. After that was lunch, then you either returned for more intensive classes, struggled with the subjunctive in the language lab, or watched an incomprehensible movie. Or you could explore Paris. If you were young and away from Mom and Dad in Paris, what would you do?

In summer it's daylight until 10:00pm, easy to lose track of time. Often they'd find themselves way across town and not able to make it home in time for dinner on the crowded Métro at rush hour. They would be forced back on the street to pay for a dinner that wasn't in Daddy's budget. And that made Daddy mad.

So, my apartment meant jailbreak. Translated: Party. And it was Friday. They gathered in groups scribbling lists, barking suggestions, and debating the menu. Odette clapped her hands for order. She handed me her dry ink marker and directed me to the board to field questions. I froze. A little history here...

When I was five, my Kindergarten teacher, a stern old crow, called my parents in for a chat. I didn't like her. I always felt she'd lost her dream job as a prison warden and had to settle for teaching five-year olds. I sat in a chair, burning with shame, making my parents come in after school.

"It has come to my attention," she began, "that your son's finger painting is not up to Kindergarten level."

My dad waited for the punch line as he and my mom shuffled through my parchments. The frustrated prison warden pointed at the dozens of smeared parchments ringing the classroom. Mine were not among them.

"His paintings don't extend to the edges like the others. His choice of colors are horrid, and there seems to be a complete lack of interest in his art."

Paintings. Art. Can you imagine? I was five.

I didn't extend to the edges because I had no interest in them. I hated the smocks, hated smearing the paint into a rainbow of sludge, while the other kids hogged all the good colors, leaving me with fuchsia and coyote brown. As we made a collective mess, all I could think of was, oh boy, after this, we get to clean this crap up. I didn't extend to the edges because I didn't want a bigger mess to clean. This all added up to, in her mind, my finger painting wasn't up to snuff for Kindergarten. Not Julliard. Kindergarten.

That day affected me to this day. I can't draw a thing, only stick figures and curvy "V"s for birds. There's no connection between what I see and what my hand draws.

So, years later in Paris, with my arm and brain paralyzed, I drew a warped circle for Paris and a frown cutting it in half, representing the Seine. As a reference point I cross-hatched some lines for the Eiffel Tower to the west.

I stepped back, horrified. It was like hanging my soiled laundry. The class was aghast, whispering to each other in horror. Odette cocked her head, then kept twisting it, hoping it would make more sense upside down. She erased it and drew a guillotine and obelisk in the center of town and wrote, "Place de la Concorde", where Marie-Antoinette lost her head. I whispered to her that I drew the Eiffel Tower, not a guillotine. She quickly erased it and drew the Tower where mine had been. I drew a shaky line for Rue de Vaugirard, then a short one intersecting it, and wrote my street name.

"Where is it?" a voice demanded from the back. Alessandra. Of course.

I drew the Métro line, but couldn't remember the stop. I scribbled the sloping park near my apartment. My disaster was complete. They'd have to figure it out themselves. This was before smartphones and GPS. They hit me from all sides. "Quand?" When?

I scribbled "samedi" on the board. Saturday.

"Non! Ce soir!" they demanded. No! Tonight!

I erased "samedi" and wrote "vendredi." They all cheered.

"Friday? That's tonight! I'm not ready!"

"Oui!"

"Yes-yes!"

"Quelle heure?" What time?

I wrote "20:00 H." 8:00pm.

"Trop tard!" Too late! They were young.

I wrote "18:00H." 6:00pm. That worked for them, not me. I'd have a lot to do.

"Quelle correspondance?" Where do we change lines?

"Wait!" I scribbled faster.

"Quelle sortie?" Which exit?

"Slow down!" I yelled.

"Quel est le menu?" What's the menu?

I whipped around. I could only take one question at a time, and they were bugging me. "Attendez!" I yelled. "Une question à la fois! Ça m'énerve! Merde!," basically telling them to shut up.

They froze like scolded children. It was my first complete sentence in French. Angry, rude French, but French nonetheless. It arced from a dusty memory bank deep in my brain and shot out. Odette, sly as a fox, had transformed a mundane vocabulary drill into a lively party planning exercise. And she got me to speak. If you can call it that.

Alessandra, who could take me down in an alley fight, raised a polite hand. "Pasta?" she almost whispered.

"Bon." I wrote it down. She and Isobel would bring pasta and salad, but she wouldn't have time to make her sauce. At least that's what I thought she said. I wrote "sauce" by my name. There was an Italian food store whose aromas could make you walk into a pole. Molly lived near a boulangerie that won the Best Baguette in Paris award. The line would be long, but she'd be happy to wait. I wrote it down. Isobel asked if she could bring her sister Ana. I didn't know Ana.

"Yes, you do," Silvia said in perfect English. "She pulled your foot out of a bucket in the broom closet." Oh, that Ana. Okay, she could come.

Sandra wanted to bring Caroline and Martina, whoever they were. Cuky wanted to bring her roommates. Juan wanted to bring Ignacio, who would bring his German friend Didi, his personal German translator. Ignacio had a thing for one of the Swiss girls in Room 8, and Didi was the go-between.

On it went until everyone was bringing someone, or something to eat. Except Markus. We thought it best if he didn't handle food.

Odette let us out early. We blasted out of there like, well, kids out of school. I had a lot to do before six. Soon they would be pounding on my door ready for fun.

The Customer is Always Wrong

Normally I have the social habits of a hermit crab, but I was excited about my first party in Paris. I entered the Italian food store just off Boulevard Saint-Germain. Emboldened with my outburst in French, I anticipated a lively discussion. But in Paris, I was learning quickly, things rarely go as expected.

In the States for a party, we buy in bulk at a Costco or similar big box store, where they pack it up neatly for you. We throw it in the trunk and haul it home. In France, not so much.

First off, they don't have big box stores. They have their version of it in the outlying regions, but you'd have to rent a car to get it all home. The French have no interest in the economies of scale. You're limited with what you can lug home in two hands.

I leaned over the counter looking for someone to wait on me. The only other person in the place was an elderly woman sitting at a window table reading *La Repubblica*. I didn't know if she worked there, so I cleared my throat over and over until she realized I wasn't going away. She slammed her paper down and came over, grumbling.

"Bonjour" I said, with an air that nothing could ruin this perfect day.

"Buongiorno," she snapped, as if correcting me.

Italian.

She seemed to still be fuming over circumstances that landed her in France, far from her native, and vastly superior, Italy. But that was her problem on this beautiful Friday afternoon. I was throwing my first party in Paris.

She twirled her hand impatiently, like "get on with it." I pointed to the large simmering pot of sauce behind her.

"Sauce?" I asked. She eyed me up and down, debating whether to sell to me, or call the authorities. She held up a cup that would hold a golf ball. I spread my arms to show I needed a lot. She held up another. Two golf balls. I pointed to a stack of cups the size of a small soda at a fast-food joint.

"Six, s'il vous plaît. Non, huit." Six wouldn't do. I needed eight. Big night.

She shook her head in disgust, like I was taking food from her children, if she had any, with that attitude. I could be wrong, but wasn't she in the business of selling sauce? She slopped eight containers to the brim. I paid.

Several customers breezed in. She waited on them without an ounce of hostility. She sliced their salamis and wrapped their pastas with care, even tied a ribbon around the bag, and they breezed out. She returned to her newspaper.

If I lived upstairs from this place I could have carried the mess home without much spillage. But lugging eight uncovered cups onto the Métro was out of the question, not to mention the stairs, turnstiles, and crowds. I'd spill every drop before I got home. As I was learning, in Paris you choose your battles. I decided to take this one on.

"Excuse me?" I mimed covering the cups. "Sorry to be a pain. Lids? Odd, I know, but we Americans like our lids."

She slammed her paper down and stomped to the storage room. She came back with four mismatched lids. Four, not eight. I popped them on, but they didn't fit right, and the sides were already softening from the heat. She was already back at her paper.

"How is this going to help me?" I asked, as obnoxiously as possible. She rifled under the counter and handed me a crumpled sheet of used plastic wrap and a stapler. She had a stapler, but no lids. In a store that sells sauce to go. "You want me to staple this to the cups? Really?"

She mulled my logic. She scrounged under the counter. *Finally I'm getting through to her. See? All it took was a little patience...*

She slapped a tape dispenser on the counter. Apparently, I can irritate people regardless of where they come from. It's a gift, I guess. I taped the cellophane over the tops, purposely sloshing sauce. She drummed her fingers on the counter, waiting for my next inevitable request.

"Box?" I drew a box in the air and mimed putting the cups in it. She dug around below decks and handed me a produce box. With a hole in the bottom. Service with a scowl.

I put seven cups in, thinking I'd dump the eighth on her head on the way out, then reconsidered. I cradled the bottom with one arm and steadied the cups with the other and sloshed out to the street. By the time I got to the bus stop I looked like a murder scene.

When the bus arrived I assumed the other passengers would give me room to negotiate the steps, with the blood and all. But when the doors opened it was one for all, and all at once. I was knocked and spun around until I stumbled back to the sidewalk. When I finally got on, even though I'd ridden the same bus with the same driver all week, he insisted I show him my pass.

"Really? You want me to put this mess down?" He gestured, show it, or get off. With passengers pushing past me, I set the box down, happy it leaked on his floor, and flashed my pass. Before I could pick the box up, the bus lurched forward, spilling more sauce.

There was no place to sit. Everyone had placed their coats and purses in the empty seats beside them, looking out the window. So I stood all the way home, one bloody arm under the box, the other wrapped around a pole to steady myself in the lurching Paris traffic.

When I stepped off, I noticed Parisians effortlessly carrying their groceries in two bags, with children in tow. *How do they do it?* When I got to my apartment I collapsed in the kitchen, exhausted.

It took two and a half hours, all I had was sauce, and people would be showing up in less than an hour. I changed my shirt and headed back down to my local market.

I grabbed some wine, cheese, and various things. The cashier rang me up, but before I could pay, she shoved everything aside and started ringing up the next customer. She shoved so hard a wine bottle bounced over the side. If I hadn't caught it, it would have shattered. Service with a shove.

I waited for someone to bag them, but the next customer's groceries were shoved on top of mine. She sifted through the rubble and tossed her stuff into her bags and left. I scooped everything up and walked home angry. But you know what? Next time I'll bring bags.

I was looking forward to the evening. A week ago I was sleeping on a bone-crunching wood floor in a stranger's apartment who wanted me out as soon as possible. Now I was hosting a party in my own place.

****

As I was pouring Signora's sauce into a pot, Alessandra and Silvia appeared in the kitchen doorway. They plopped grocery bags full of tomatoes, peppers, onions, and various spices on my small table. I had misunderstood them in class. Oh well, plenty of sauce for all. They gave me the "get out of your kitchen" look. As I turned to leave, I looked right over tiny Ana to Isobel, who arrived with some friends. Silvia raided my cabinets and plopped more pots on the stove.

There was a steady flow of arriving guests. I didn't know most of them, but they all brought something and couldn't thank me enough for inviting them, which I hadn't, most of them, anyway. I was pleased that Yoko came. She was so shy in class, and possibly the only one who spoke less French than me.

The guests I knew were relaxed, laughing, and joking, something we didn't have time for while conjugating verbs. I understood why they brought friends. Like me, their brains were knotted up from French. They wanted to speak their own language and unwind. I did too. Banned from my own kitchen, I grabbed some wine and headed to the living room.

It was quite a sight. Everyone had settled on the floor, sofa, and the few chairs I had. Languages floated around the room; Italian, German, English, Japanese, Flemish, and Spanish. A few braves ones attempted French. Ana tromped through with her foot-in-bucket routine, to everyone's delight, except mine.

Stories were told. Laughter boomed from various groups. I was glad to hear I wasn't the only one making mistakes. Some were hilarious, others embarrassing, but it was all in good fun. We knew better than to laugh at someone else's expense. We'd be the victim soon enough.

Isobel found good music on the radio. Didi interpreted for Ignacio and the pretty Swiss girl. Alessandra added spices to the sauce. It made us swoon, and our stomachs growl.

There was a commotion in the bathroom. Silvia and Ana shoved past me to get there first. Those two, always in the thick of it. When I entered, everyone was jostling for position at the window.

The Eiffel Tower was glowing amber across town. Someone would get a five-second view of it before being yanked away by someone who wanted in on the action. Ana couldn't see, so she stepped onto the rim of the tub, then crawled onto Juan's shoulders. I don't think he even noticed.

The Tower galvanized them. They dropped their mother tongues and spoke in hushed French.

"Magnifique..."

"Formidable..."

"Merveilleux..."

Alessandra boomed in wondering what the commotion was about. She tossed people out of the way like rag dolls and looked out the window. "Che bellissima!" she almost sang, then returned to the kitchen.

Everyone had a story about the Tower; the first time they saw it, first time they went to the top, and their first kiss under it.

Ana presided over the whole thing on Juan's shoulders like a school master. For the first time in her life, she was taller than everyone, and she used it to full advantage. If someone hogged the view, she'd grab them by the collar and pull them back.

I sat on the tub and marveled. I was having a party in my bathroom! How many can say that? They all spoke better than me, so I was content to listen. Maybe all language classes should be taught in bathrooms.

Like thunder in the night, Alessandra's voice boomed from the kitchen. Silvia and I rushed out. The burners on the stove had gone out. The pasta water was cold, but

Alessandra was boiling. I sniffed for gas. I opened the oven to check the pilot light. Nothing. This must have been what the concierge was trying to tell me.

Ana crawled through my legs and popped up to scope out the situation. She banged the butane tank with a ladle. It clanged like a school bell. Empty.

The news spread like wildfire and soon the kitchen was crammed with hungry onlookers. Alessandra's anger singed my neck. How in the world would I swap out a butane tank on a Friday night in Paris?

Before I could figure out a plan, Isobel grabbed the pot and dashed out the door. Alessandra followed with her sauce. Silvia and Ana ran to catch up. I chased after them and watched in horror as Isobel kicked a neighbor's door, sloshing water onto the hall floor.

Bam! Bam! Bam! No one home. Another door.

Bam! Bam! Bam! She marched upstairs.

Bam! Bam! Bam! I was sure I would get kicked out of the building. Then I heard a door open, and female conversation. Silvia hollered down the stairwell. I dashed up to the next floor and entered an apartment.

In the kitchen Silvia, Isobel, Ana, and Alessandra were talking with a young woman who was wiping her hands on her apron. Our pasta water and sauce were heating up on her stove. On the other two burners she was cooking her dinner.

"Bonsoir, monsieur!" she said. "Marie-Hélène." She shook my hand then escorted me into the living room where her husband Roland sat reading the paper. He was as surprised as I was. Marie-Hélène told him to pour me a drink, which I needed.

I recognized them. They were the couple I saw walking arm in arm in the courtyard when I met with Laurie. They were newlyweds, struggling in their early years together. Wedding pictures everywhere. Roland poured me a glass of wine and motioned for me to sit down. He was still in his suit from work. We had taken over their home and ruined their Friday night together.

"Américain?" Roland asked. I nodded.

"California." His face filled with wonder.

"Someday, but..." He rubbed his fingers together. No money. His English was about as good as my French, so we just sipped. We're guys. But in the kitchen the five women were talking like there was no tomorrow. And there might not be if I didn't get dinner served.

Roland showed me their wedding photos. He was so proud of her. "One year tomorrow. Anniversaire." And they were spending it cooking someone else's dinner. Sheesh.

The fresh pasta only needed a few minutes. Soon, Alessandra dashed past with her sauce, Silvia with the pasta, Isobel held the door open, and Ana yelled something at me that sounded like "Get the lead out." I thanked them and left, making a mental note to do something for their anniversary.

When I got back, there was a line out of the kitchen and into the living room. Guests were coming out with plates of pasta, salad, bread, and wine in my mismatched glasses. Alessandra accepted kudos for her sauce. She had skillfully mixed in Signora's sauce with hers. It was beyond delicious.

Our brains were mush from school, so we ate in silence. Molly's baguettes sopped up the sauce, bottles of red and white wine were passed around. We ate like kings and queens. Ignacio reserved the bathroom window, dinner for two. Didi interpreted sitting on the tub. She was impressed.

My wall map of Paris turned out to be the hit of the evening. Everyone took their turn in front of it. They traced fingers across it, learning Paris from a bird's eye view. There wasn't a moment the entire evening when there weren't at least four people searching for something on it.

The evening flew by. The Métro had long since closed, so there was a line to use my phone to call a cab. Judging from the cursing, they weren't having much luck. I just wanted my bed, but there were three people curled up on it for the night.

I wasn't about to send anyone home at this hour. They'd be locked out of their host families anyway. They ransacked my wardrobe for blankets, sheets, towels, anything they could find. There wasn't much, but everyone found something to curl up with. And just like that, they were in for the night.

I shut the music off and went to brush my teeth and wash my face. I didn't notice until on the way out that Ana was in the tub sound asleep, a rolled up towel as her pillow. I turned off the light and shut the door.

The next morning my apartment looked like a war zone, or an orgy, bodies everywhere, dirty dishes and wine bottles strewn about. I snuck out and bought out the left side of the pâtisserie shelves and a couple baguettes. By the time I got home Silvia had washed a few plates to put them on.

Bodies rose and stretched like the waking dead. They trudged to the bathroom door and pounded. Ana had to give up her private suite.

It was slow going heating up espressos two at a time. I put out some cartons of juice and milk. It wasn't much, but everyone was careful not to take too much. We ate quietly. Everyone cleaned up. Some left, some stayed, but they all took a last peek out the window. The Tower was different in daylight, like it was asleep, shrouded in haze.

By noon, everyone was gone. And that's when I realized how tired I was. It was jet lag. It was being back in a classroom. It was struggling to communicate in a beautiful, but difficult, language. It was frustration. It was exhaustion.

There was an inch of wine left in a bottle. The pastries were gone, but I found some stale bread from the previous night. I sat on the window sill, one leg hanging out. I tore off chunks and dipped it in the wine. I stared at the Tower for an hour. When I finished, desperately needing sleep, I staggered out of the bathroom. I don't remember making it to the bed.

A Nuit Blanche

The phone woke me out of a deep sleep. I reeled in the cord and answered. "Allo? C'est Framboise."

"Who?"

"Crêpe Grand Marnier."

"Oh, you." I didn't mean it that way. She ignored it. Again, the French.

"We go to cinema tonight. You come?"

The thought of spending an evening with Framboise and strangers was terrifying. I could fake French with my classmates, but with a seasoned veteran like her, and strangers, it would be difficult. I was too fuzzy brained to think of an excuse, so I scribbled her address and Métro stop and hung up.

But I had to do something first. I walked to the corner wine shop and bought a bottle of Champagne. I placed it at Roland and Marie-Hélène's door with a card thanking them for the cooking, and wishing them a happy anniversary.

After a deep sleep, I was looking forward to the evening. I had been in Paris a week, and being invited out with Parisian friends was overwhelming. I met up with

Framboise and her friends. One guy, Jean-François, couldn't wait to tell me about his favorite place to eat.

The movie and dinner experience is different in Paris. In the States, we choose a time, then back time it to when we should eat, factor in the time to get to the cinema, and still have time buy popcorn before we finally sit.

However, when we gathered, there was no discussion of which movie, what time, or even when or where to eat. Rather, we strolled along Boulevard Saint-Germain, to Saint-Michel, and across the Seine past Nôtre Dame. In the Parisian way, we were passing time until the ten o'clock show.

Even though I sat in the theater, I can't say I saw the movie, rather I stared at the screen for two hours. It was a French movie, no subtitles. I had no idea what it was about, other than a bunch of people entered and exited, slamming doors and ignoring each other.

Well past midnight, we dined at an outdoor café. Jean-François pouted, having been outvoted for dinner at his favorite chicken sandwich joint. So, after dinner we piled into someone's car, zoomed over the Pont Alexander III, a bridge over the Seine, and careened down a narrow street to the famed chicken joint.

Jean-François ordered the #1, which was chicken with mayo wrapped in a soggy bun. I didn't want to break his heart, but it was nothing any fast-food joint in the States couldn't whip up at a moment's notice. But Jean-François loved it. We sat on outdoor benches and got a kick out of him savoring every soggy bite. But I'll always remember that night for something else.

After Jean-François tossed the greasy remains in the trash, no one spoke. They were listening to the silence, lost in their thoughts. The Tower had gone to sleep hours ago. No motos whizzed by, no sirens. Paris was in a deep sleep. I thought back to nights in bed when there wasn't a moment I didn't hear something slicing the silence. But right then there was none of it.

"It only lasts a few minutes," Jean-François whispered. The silence made me realize how my life had changed so quickly. It seemed so long ago I struggled with suitcases and intercoms and crêpes, and now I was listening to Paris sleep, with friends.

And just like that, a new day began. A nuit blanche, a white night, where you stay up all night and witness Paris waking up.

An elderly woman opened her door and took her dog for a walk. Down the street, a car door opened and shut. Its engine started and it roared off.

Up high, a window scraped open. A woman in a terrific flimsy nightgown stretched, and inhaled the cool predawn air. In an hour or two she'd be turning heads on the street, but right now she was all yawns and puffy eyes. A man came up behind her and gently pulled her away. They'd be late for work.

The ground rumbled through my shoes like a distant earthquake. The Métro was open for business. We could feel the cars bumping into position. Soon people would be inhaling their last puff before descending into the tunnels.

"Sometimes I stay out all night to hear the silence," Jean-François said, "then I take the Métro home in the morning."

By the time we piled into the cars, the smell of baking bread filled the streets. It was comforting to know the French could bake croissants faster than I could eat them, but I had them working twenty-four hours a day.

They dropped me off and we made arrangements to rendezvous soon. I dashed across the street and bought a croissant and pain au chocolat.

When I got back to my floor, Roland was tiptoeing downstairs. He thanked me for the Champagne. He was ashamed he couldn't buy Marie-Hélène an anniversary gift, but when they found the Champagne, they made a plan. He popped and poured, she made a bubble bath.

They soaked in the tub until the bottle was empty, then made love deep into the night. It was, in his words, *parfait*. Perfect.

He was sneaking out to surprise her with some pastries. Later he left a note at my door, thanking me, saying I shouldn't hesitate to call if I ever needed help again. I still have that card. Everyone should drink more Champagne.

****

As the weeks rolled by, we hung out on the terrace between classes and discussed our struggles. I felt I was at a disadvantage with the Spaniards and Italians. But I learned it's a fallacy to think if someone speaks a Latin-based language, they'll pick up another one easily. I would argue the opposite.

An Italian feminine noun might be masculine in French or Spanish, or vice-versa. A transitive French verb might be intransitive in Italian or Spanish and not take a preposition. Or the preposition used could be different in all three. You have to learn them all. People who say it's easy never studied a foreign language.

But none of us had Yoko's problem. One day I found her in the school lobby pouring over her notes, almost in tears. We all liked her so much, invited her to everything, but we could see she was struggling, worse than me, if possible.

Not only was she destined for a loveless, arranged marriage when she returned to Japan, her last hope of some fun in Paris wasn't turning out like she planned.

She didn't understand English, so I gestured, asking if I could help her. She gathered her things and led me downstairs to a hall of classrooms I didn't know existed. In one, a teacher was speaking slow, deliberate French. The class was entirely Asian.

They had stunned looks on their faces. The teacher drew a large "P" and a small "p" on the board. The struggling students traced the letters with stencils. Yoko, and this class, couldn't learn French until they learned our alphabet.

From that day forward, I never looked at my problems the same way. Every time I struggled with the imperfect past tense, I thought of that class tracing letters. She should have been in it, but wanted to stay with us even if it meant learning almost nothing. I felt honored she let me in on her secret. She never told anyone else, and neither did I.

Dumped at the Concorde

Even in Paris the classroom can get boring, so we signed up for a tour of the Peugeot factory. We walked a few blocks to Boulevard Saint-Germain and hopped on a chartered bus.

We zoomed across the Périphérique and into the suburbs. We stuck our heads out the window like dogs. We watched the Tower and the Arc and Sacré Cœur fade in the distance. It did us all good. Except Juan. He was homesick for Madrid. I tried to distract him by asking him what a traffic sign meant.

"How should I know?" he grumbled. "It's in French."

We were herded into the factory like prisoners and issued protective goggles that fogged up immediately. Ana's almost covered her entire face, making her look like a giant wasp. We tripped over each other going up a flight of stairs, cursing in our native tongues.

We toured the factory for two hours and didn't learn a thing. We couldn't hear the guide over the pounding of the assembly line machinery, and couldn't see a thing.

I may have not learned anything from the tour, but I sure did on the ride back. Parisians are big on improvisation. I think that's why they love jazz so much. It's the only way to explain why we were picked up on Boulevard Saint-Germain, but on the return were dumped in the middle of six lanes of roaring traffic on the Place de la Concorde.

The brakes hissed and the doors flew open. Odette stepped off and waved us to follow, as if it were a walk in the park. Silvia piped in with her opinion before disembarking. Markus looked at me, "Yes-yes!" and shambled off. The rest of us followed, right into the middle of the Indy 500.

We huddled like scared chickens as the bus blew a black cloud of diesel fumes on us. Odette circled us like a mother hen. We'd get moving one way, then a car would whiz past and blow us back.

Then Olga screamed, "Par là!" This way!

We darted through a hole in the traffic and hurried into the underground walkway, and popped up on Rue de Rivoli. Without Yoko.

She was still out there, staring down the oncoming traffic. Suddenly, she sprinted into it like a jackrabbit on fire. Horns honked and tires screeched, but she took on all comers. She zigged one way, then spun on a dime the other way. Twice we thought she'd bought the farm, but she was like a bull taking on a hundred red capes.

"Run, Yoko, run!" we yelled in six languages.

Yoko faked out a Vespa that skittered into the Tuileries, taking out a souvenir stand. A truck barreled down on her, but she spun away at the last second. Her chest was heaving, adrenaline roaring through her veins, and judging from her smile, was having the time of her life.

She waved to us. We waved back. What else could we do? She shot in front of a car, whacked its hood, and sprinted toward us. The guys couldn't look, but the girls cheered her on. A truck swerved around her, as she ran headlong into our arms and collapsed in a heap, with a smile as bright as the sun. She was fine. We were a mess. How could she return to Japan and marry that dolt after a death run across the Concorde?

When a classmate gives you a fright like that, there's only one place to go; Café Angelina for hot chocolate. Yoko led the way. We shoved tables together to make room. Normally that's a no-no, but after the waiters heard of Yoko's heroics they brought us each a Kir, white wine with a splash of crème de cassis to get things going. Perfect.

Yoko recounted her exploit with a little Japanese, a little French, and a lot of laughing. We were just happy she was alive. We toasted her brush with death with an "à santé," to life! Which she thankfully still had.

Some Friendly Advice

One evening we went to a party at an English couple's apartment. They were students in our school who worked for the British Council, and stationed in Paris. Since they were diplomats, they were set up in a swanky apartment on Île Saint-Louis. Lucky them, lucky us.

There are two islands in the Seine. The more busy and popular is the Île de la Cité, home of the Préfecture de Police, Palais de Justice, Hôtel Dieu, and of course Nôtre Dame. But just behind it, connected by a pedestrian bridge, is the quieter and très chic, Île Saint-Louis.

It was a beautiful apartment, and the couple had gone all out for us. I recognized a lot of the faces, friends who had tagged along to my party. A few came over and thanked me again. In fact, they pointed out, I was becoming quite well-known, thanks to Ana, who was at it again with her bucket routine, having found a new audience for her act.

Alessandra entertained a group with the empty butane tank story. Silvia mimed Isobel kicking doors while holding the pasta pot. Odette told a group about an oral exam where the student had been drinking. I countered that I only had one glass. Odette twisted her hand on her nose, the French sign for "drunk." The only one missing was Framboise with her Crêpe Grand Marnier story.

I struck up a conversation with one of the other teachers at school. She asked me how Paris was treating me. I told her about our return trip to the Concorde, and Yoko's brush with death. I was impressed how effortlessly I recounted the story, weaving through the present, past, and conditional tenses, until I realized I was speaking English. And so was she. "I can't speak a word of French," I said.

"I heard you told your class to shut up," she said, with obvious delight. That was true, I told her, but it was in a fit of rage. I could start a sentence okay, but then I'd trip up on verb tenses and prepositions. Or I'd forget a word that I'd looked up a hundred times in the dictionary. She asked me to give her an example. I plowed through in my horrible French.

"I was walking down the street, and I got to the... the...," I jutted my arms crossways in front of me.

"Carrefour," she said, almost psychic. An intersection.

"Right. What's it called again?"

"Carrefour."

"Of course. I was walking down the street, and I got to the...oh, for chrissakes, what was it again?"

"Carrefour." She was so patient.

"How could I forget? Okay. I was walking down the... the..."

"Rue."

"Yes, rue. Street. I was walking...

"Why don't you tell me English," she interrupted. "I have a doctor's appointment next Thursday. I don't want to miss it."

She explained my brain was in a knot and it needed to relax. She suggested after classes finished I go to a country where I didn't know the language. I pointed out I was already in one.

"Just forget everything you've learned," she said.

"Done."

She explained learning a language is a lifelong pursuit. You can study until the cows come home, but you'll always make mistakes. But it seemed my cows had jumped the fence, never to return.

Her husband was South African, his native language English, but he spoke perfect French. She was French, and spoke perfect English. Their two jobs and home couldn't have been farther apart. To break up the monotony of commuting alone, they often met at an agreed-upon café for dinner, so they could ride home together. But at least once a month, they ended up sitting at different cafés waiting for the other one, who never showed up. Swapping between English and French inevitably caused miscommunication, even after more than twenty-five years together.

She told the story for encouragement, but it seemed to have the opposite effect on me.

Sunday with the Boss

One Sunday evening some of us went to the Hippodrome for a Bruce Springsteen concert. Weirdest concert I'd even been to, and that includes Joe Cocker at the Hollywood Bowl, when he'd lost his voice and gyrated and twitched for two hours and nothing came out. Not a peep.

We sat on blankets and munched on bread, sausage, and cheese, washed down with some wine. A subdued voice announced on the PA system, "Mesdames et Messieurs, Monsieur Bruce Springsteen," as if it were a spelling bee.

The Boss exploded onstage, pounding his guitar while Clarence Clemons wailed on his sax. I had never seen Springsteen before. It sent chills down my spine. It was exhausting just watching him. I couldn't believe he could keep this up for his legendary four hours.

At the end of the opening number, he screamed "Thank you, thank you for coming!" To utter silence.

After a few seconds, there was a smattering of polite applause. This ran counter to everything I'd ever heard about a Springsteen concert, where fans were on their feet, singing and dancing in the aisles. Here, you could hear a pin drop.

It was uncomfortable with these awkward, silent gaps between the songs. I would instinctively applaud after each song, then temper it, so I didn't offend anyone. Europeans, and the French in particular, enjoy the music inwardly, as opposed to us crazy Americans who pull out all the stops. Every review I read, and person I talked to who had been there, drooled their love for The Boss and his show at the Hippodrome. They just didn't show it.

Late, Right on Time

School and summer were over. We'd planned a picnic at Chateau Versailles, and that would be last time I would see most of my classmates. We had laughed and teased each other shamelessly, but there was always another class, more laughs, more rendezvous.

But something bothered me about the odd start time ever since we had planned it. Deux heures. Why two o'clock? It was the last time we'd all be together. Wouldn't we want to spend as much time together as possible? Many would be leaving that evening.

I was tumbling all this over in my mind on the bus to Versailles. It's a nice ride out there. I like buses. As efficient as the Métro is, it takes longer to get oriented because you're underground, and then you pop up all over the city like a gopher. On a bus you see everything and your brain maps it. But the deux heures thing still bothered me because I didn't see anyone from class on the bus.

As I approached Versailles, I saw them lined up at the stop. How thoughtful, I thought. Sandra saw me first, and she wasn't smiling. None of them were. They looked like they were about to riot. I couldn't wait to find out what the problem was. Maybe I could help.

They swarmed me as I stepped off. Little Ana wagged her finger in my face yelling in Spanish. Silvia and Alessandra lit into me in Italian, Sandra in German. Even shy Molly got into the act, all yelling like a pack of wild dogs, tapping their watches.

Didi, always the diplomat, pulled me aside and asked why I was two hours late. I pointed out I arrived at deux heures. That's all it took. He went over to the group and explained. They calmed down a bit, but not much.

Our picnic was planned for *douze* heures, twelve o'clock, not *deux*, two o'clock. The difference is subtle, like "accept" and "except." But to my concrete ears, I hadn't heard the difference, thought the picnic was at two o'clock, and promptly arrived two hours late. Merde.

They were still grumbling when we arrived at the Chateau and searched for the perfect picnic spot. They weren't angry, they were hungry. We found a spot on the grass near the entrance. What a backdrop! The women were still simmering as we ate and drank. They couldn't accept the fact that I'm genetically inclined to mistakes. But the men had, and already forgotten about it.

I hadn't talked to Didi much before, he was always busy translating for Ignacio. I thanked him for rescuing me, and we became fast friends. And, he could speak with the cute German and Swiss girls. Always a plus.

There was plenty of sunlight, but not plenty of time. After our picnic everyone would return to Paris and pack for their journeys back home. We laughed, told stories about our mistakes in class, and laughed some more. Ana couldn't resist one more clomping across the grass. Talented, that Ana is.

And just like that, we got uncomfortably quiet. Everyone checked their watches. Without a word we picked up everything and headed for the bus stop.

We rode the bus back to Paris in silence, deep in our thoughts while looking out the window. We made sure we all had copies of our addresses and phone numbers. And yes, we would keep in touch. Ana plopped down next to me. I looked down at the top of her head. She looked up.

"Merci," she said. Ana felt we all had become good friends the night the butane tank let us down. Having to figure out what to do, meeting Roland and Marie-Hélène, the food and wine, the Tower out my bathroom window, everyone staying over and cleaning up the next morning. And she got to sleep in the tub.

"Tout était parfait," she said. Everything was perfect.

We stepped off the bus and stood awkwardly, waiting for someone to say something. Finally someone hugged, and we all joined in. We exchanged four-cheek kisses. Two simply wouldn't do for a final good-bye. We all hugged again. My eyes burned. I thought about who I would miss the most, but couldn't decide. We descended into the Métro and scattered to various lines. No one turned around.

I went home and didn't know what to do. The pressure of learning forged intense friendships so quickly, it left us exhausted. I sat in the kitchen, hatching a scheme from some conversations I heard at the picnic. With a little luck it might work.

I would meet Juan at Gare d'Austerlitz for his train to Madrid, then dash over to Gare de Lyon to say good-bye to Alessandra and Silvia who were returning to Italy.

I checked the departure board and made it just in time to knock on Juan's window as his train pulled away. He poked his chest, pointed at me, then south. He'd see me in Madrid. Juan was terrific. I grabbed the Métro and headed to Gare de Lyon.

I found Alessandra and Silvia sitting on their suitcases on the platform, staring at the ground. I studied them from a distance. They had changed. They arrived in Paris for the summer as giggly girls. At the end they were women. Paris does that. What would it do to me?...

A crowd surged past them as their train pulled in. They didn't want to leave. For a moment I thought they wouldn't board. But when the whistle blew, their time in Paris had ended.

Silvia dragged her suitcase toward the car but couldn't lift it. She stepped aboard but couldn't pull it in. Alessandra couldn't push it in. They panicked when the whistle blew again.

I stepped in front of Alessandra and heaved Silvia's suitcase up and in. I grabbed Alessandra's and threw it in. She hopped over it and pulled it in. Relieved they made it, they blurted, "Merci, monsieur!"

When they saw it was me, they froze. Alessandra pushed against the swarm of boarding passengers and hopped off the train. She bear-hugged me and told me, threatened really, that I must come to Italy and learn Italian. I was having enough trouble with one foreign language, I couldn't fathom another one. Maybe some day.

She demanded that I promise or she wouldn't release me, and I believed her. I nodded. She told me Ana was right. "Tout était parfait," she said.

"Oui, tout était parfait, Alessandra. Au revoir."

"Au revoir."

She hopped on the train. I walked alongside as the train pulled out of the station. They blew kisses from their window as they sped away. I can still feel those kisses today.

When their train left the station, the first phase of my life in Paris was over. My formal education was finished. I had studied all summer, but only dogs and three-year olds understood me.

We had partied at my apartment, dined and watched movies all over Paris, picnicked at Versailles, drank Champagne in Epernay, wandered Monet's home and gardens in Giverny, almost got killed at the Concorde, drank hot chocolate at Café Angelyne, learned nothing about Peugeots, argued, but also laughed and teased each other relentlessly, and spoke a little French along the way. And now it was over.

Being in those train stations made me want to travel. That teacher was right. I needed to get out of Paris for a while. When I got home I unfolded a map and connected the dots of places and friends I wanted to visit. Germany, Switzerland, Italy, and who knows where else?

It felt odd wanting to leave Paris. I only had so much time there, and now some of it would be spent away. I had the luxury of not having to travel in late summer, when all of Europe is on vacation, and backpackers from all over the world filled the trains. Besides, another opportunity arose.

Snails & Dominique

An aunt back home wrote me to suggest I meet an American friend of a friend living in Paris. I was less than enthusiastic because of my last experience meeting a friend of a friend, but in the end, I agreed.

Ann wrote the food article for an airline magazine. What's more, she lived in Saint-Michel. I'd always admired the apartments straddling Rues Saint-Michel and Danton. Now was a chance to see one.

When I exited the Métro at Saint Michel I felt different. I looked around. The cafés were filling up on this Saturday evening. Lovers cuddled, and children splashed them at the Fountain. Horns honked. Crowds flowed into the Latin Quarter.

I thought back, this is where I arrived, struggling with my luggage, perspiring in my wool coat, feeling lost, even though I had a destination.

Everything was difficult in the beginning, but things had smoothed out. Sure, inconveniences popped up at times, but overall I was hitting my stride. And I loved it.

I'd made friends, local and foreign. I'd see some of them soon. My money was holding out okay, but I had to watch it carefully.

I had a few minutes before meeting Ann, so I walked onto the Saint Michel bridge over the Seine. A young couple asked me to take their picture. Two French girls walked past. One was upset that a guy she met hadn't called her. Her friend advised her to play hard to get. Some things are universal. It was fun to understand them.

I watched Bateaux Mouches, those big dinner boats that ply the Seine, pass under me. The waiters were making last minute checks of the tables that would soon be filled with hungry passengers. I loved watching them, but I had to meet Ann. I pulled myself away and walked up Rue Saint Michel. I found the address, pushed the button next to her name, and she buzzed me in.

Turned out, she was a hoot. She lived alone in a small top-floor apartment with her books and magazines piled everywhere. She lifted a stack out of the only available chair for me to sit. She had the always entertaining love/hate relationship with Paris. Everything was too small, too expensive, too difficult, too everything, but wouldn't leave for anything.

We talked easily about what brought us to Paris, what we loved and hated. She had many more of both than me, but she'd lived there longer. After an aperitif we connected the dots of what brought us together.

Then she surprised me by inviting me the following week to a private dinner at an exclusive restaurant in the 2nd arrondissement. I was flattered, but told her that wasn't my cup of tea. "Perfect!" she gushed, it wasn't hers either, but the Champagne would be fantastic!

So that's how I found myself rumbling along on the Métro with Ann, on the way to the 2nd arrondissement, all snug in my wool coat on a cool fall evening. We were greeted warmly at the door, checked our coats, and were whisked upstairs to a private dining room. She knew the other guests and introduced me around. And then I heard that wonderful music, popping Champagne corks.

It was delicious, the people were nice, and the table was perfect. We took our seats and I gazed around the table. I thought back to when I got the idea to come to Paris. Who could guess that I'd be sitting in a Michelin three-star restaurant for a private dinner?

A distinguished man, in a grey suit, welcomed us and introduced the chef, who looked almost rakish in his tailored white jacket and toque. He wished us all well and left for the kitchen to get started. We read our menu cards.

"Uh-oh," I said. I looked up from mine, then down again, hoping the words would have somehow run away. "Escargot à l'ail," I said in shock. Snails in garlic. Can you imagine? Seriously, what's the garlic going to do?

The menu explained that these six gummy gastropods had been purged, code speak for yanked out of their shells, sautéed in butter and garlic, infused with chicken stock, and covered in a garlic and thyme sauce for *une expérience unique*. It didn't mention you could cook an army boot like that and get the same result.

"You don't like snails?" Ann asked, miffed, studying my face.

"I'd rather eat a screwdriver."

"I suppose you don't eat oysters either?" she pressed.

"I won't even look at them."

Soon, plates of snails were served. It wasn't the first time I'd seen them on a plate. When I was a kid, I collected snails in the garden and placed them on a paper plate. But they were to hurl at a kid down the street I didn't like. I certainly didn't eat them. But here they were, front and center. And, my goodness, they were ugly.

When the last plate of mollusks were presented, everyone gushed, "Bon appétit!"

I had no intention of eating them, but I had a plan. I pretended to be in a lively conversation with several diners while trying to flick the critters into the floral centerpiece with my fork. But no matter how hard I flicked, they stuck firmly to the tongs. Time for Plan B.

I studied my shoes, thinking I could stuff them in there, then later dig them out and toss them in the gutter. Where they belonged, by the way. But Ann was on to me.

"Don't you dare," she warned. "We'll never be asked back."

"What's the downside of that?" I asked, staring at my snails. Realizing I'd have to eat at least a few, I studied the specially-designed tongs. I couldn't imagine someone spending their limited time on this beautiful earth designing a contraption that yanks snails out of their domestic bliss. But, I plunged in and pulled one out. It lay there like a slug. Now what?

I looked around the table. Everyone was smearing them in the sauce and lapping them up with bread, enjoying them like Skittles. Seldom do I wish ill on others, but I was hoping someone would go down for the count with a bad one, forcing the plates to be swept away in horror. Ann tapped my newly-refilled Champagne glass.

"Wash them down with some bubbly. If you wait too long, the butter will curdle in your stomach." Ann, with the pep talk.

No matter how I re-arranged them, there were still six of them. One or two I could hide under some bread, but there were too many. And they were big. I tried to form an image in my head, as far removed from where I was to distract me from what I was eating. I settled on penguins in pork pie hats visiting the Sphinx on an even-numbered Thursday.

I held my breath, shoved one in, and downed my entire Champagne. I almost blacked out as it fizzed up into my nose, blinding me. When my sight came back, I looked at my plate. Couldn't do it again.

The chef came out to gather his first-course accolades. Of course, he started down our side of the table. Panicked, I tossed two snails in my mouth and downed all of Ann's Champagne.

"Hey!"

One slug snagged on a tonsil, the other on a molar. The chef inched closer. I swirled my tongue to dislodge it. It broke loose and parked itself on the other tonsil.

"Eh, monsieur?" I spun around. The chef was smiling down at me waiting for--can you imagine?--a compliment on his snails. When my sinuses stopped burning, I gulped the filthy slugs into my stomach.

Ann reached around me. I heard the *ting-ting-ting* of her stabbing fork on my plate. She dabbed her mouth, telling the chef the snails were *fantastique*! He smiled and moved on. Ann had eaten all but one of mine.

"You should give them another try. They aren't bad." Not bad for snails, I'm sure she meant. "You shouldn't leave them on your plate in a place like this."

She had a point. This was haute-cuisine at its haughtiest. I needed more bubbly. But our glasses were empty, and the sommelier was bringing in matching wine for the next course. But the lady to my left had a full glass. I'd heard her speaking English earlier, so I thought I'd give it a try.

I pointed to her half-filled Champagne flute. "Are you going to finish that?" I asked, as casually as I could.

"Pardon?" She was sure she misunderstood.

"Otherwise," I patted my belly, "up they come."

She quickly slid her glass over. I tossed it back. It foamed violently in my mouth. I tossed in the last snot clod and swallowed, repressing a gag.

"They're interesting, aren't they?" Ann asked.

"I can think of another word," I said, "a few, actually," as I rattled my head to shake loose the image of what was sliding into my stomach.

Menu cards were passed around for the next course. I didn't think lightning could strike twice, but mushrooms were up next, a tick below snails on my gag-o-meter.

"What's the matter with mushrooms?" she asked, reading my face.

"What's so special about something a pig can find?

"Those are truffles, and I think they're delicious" Ann countered.

"They're a fungus. You don't eat fungus, you eradicate it."

Fortunately the mushrooms were only the side dish for a delicious poached whitefish wrapped in cucumber lasagna. It was matched with a crisp, white Burgundy, minerally, sharp on the tongue. A few gulps smoothed out the rough edges of the evening, and the meal.

Other than Ann, I didn't know anyone at the table, but they were a chatty bunch, and genuinely interested in why I was in Paris. The desserts rolled in on an elaborate cart. Ann instructed I could take more than one, but must make sure I ate it. The French don't understand leftovers. We finished off with cognac and espresso. Snails and mushrooms not withstanding, it was an exquisite evening.

But none of it could compare to Dominique, the hatcheck girl downstairs. We had been whisked upstairs so quickly I only got a glimpse of her checking coats. But a glimpse was all it took.

It was with her on my mind when Ann and I went down to retrieve our coats before leaving. I was a bit tipsy from power gulping the Champagne, various wines, and cognac, but the thought of seeing Dominique again put my senses on high alert.

I handed her my number card. "It has a shoeprint on the shoulder. Probably the only coat that does," I said in French. I had been rehearsing the line since the whitefish. I wanted to sound helpful, yet direct, and interested.

She smiled professionally when she handed it to me, then looked past me to the next customer. My arm raised in that familiar tick, index finger pointing skyward, to make my next point.

"Uh..."

"Oui, monsieur?" she asked, as she handed someone their coat and took another card.

I casually mentioned I had eaten two snails upstairs, like a skydiver or glacier skier might, thinking it would impress her.

"Très bien, monsieur." She reached past me and handed out another coat.

"Uh..." Finger still pointing skyward.

"Oui?" she asked, staring past me. I was causing a traffic jam at her booth. To my right, the distinguished man in the grey suit from upstairs glared at me. "Ca va, Dom?" he asked her, wanting to know if everything was all right.

"Oui, Papa," she assured him.

Papa?

Then the chef, still in his chef's jacket and toque, appeared from the left. They flanked her like two security guards. "Ca va, Dominique?" the chef asked.

"Oui, oncle, ça va," she replied.

Uncle?

I'm usually wrong in these situations, but I thought I noticed something in her eye that gave me a glimmer of hope. I asked if I could return sometime to practice my French with her. She didn't say no, which, in my book meant yes, and went out of her way to point out it needed work.

It was settled, in my mind at least, I would come back and ask her out. But not tonight, not with snails in my stomach.

****

Outside I told Ann I wanted to walk home. We made plans to get together again. She had another private dinner invitation in Deauville and felt sure I would add a spark to that drab dinner affair. She descended into the Métro and I headed for a long, but much needed, walk home.

I thought about my upcoming trip, how my money was holding out, but mostly I thought about Dominique. As rain began to fall, I realized I hadn't felt that way about someone for a long time.

It rained harder when I crossed Place Vendôme, but I couldn't think of a more perfect night to walk home in the rain. Or, as the French say, under it.

I walked along the covered sidewalk on Rue de Rivoli, and past the obelisk in the middle of the Concorde. I thought about Yoko's brush with death. Where was she now? Married to some family-arranged husband, wishing she had one more shot at those cars, I bet.

The Concorde is difficult to cross in the best of circumstances, with its sheer size and constant traffic. But in the rain it's terrifying. And I was no Yoko.

I continued down Rue de Rivoli and pressed my face against the glass of Café Angelina. It was dark and empty, but I could see and hear everything like we all were there again. Yoko laughing, and the rest of us just happy she was alive.

I continued past the Louvre, dark and foreboding in the rain. I wasn't concerned about where I would cross the Seine to the Left Bank, so I kept walking and thought about what I'd say to Dominique when I returned.

Soon, I was in the rain again, winding through streets that changed names seemingly every block. I stopped to get my bearings. I thought I recognized a café where Framboise and I had lunch one day. But everything looked different at night. I veered onto a small street, certain I'd righted the ship.

I looked up at a street sign. I was somehow in the 11th arrondissement, miles from home. I passed intersections, statues, and churches without a clue where I was. I figured I'd either find a Métro, or be half-way to Berlin by morning.

I reached the Canal Saint-Martin, a waterway that rings the city. Somehow I'd made it to the eastern edge of Paris. Nothing to do but turn around and head west. But after a few blocks, I arrived at the Canal again. I looked around. Two million people and not one was on the street at that hour. I shook the rain out of my hair like a wet dog.

I walked until I thought my legs would fall off, then turned down a street and kept going. I walked up to a sign at the corner, hoping it would be a map or a Métro station, anything to get my bearings. It said "Paris" and pointed the other direction. I was in the suburbs. I turned around and kept walking.

I was about ready to set up camp for the night on a bench when I saw a faint light glowing up ahead. It had to be a bar or pharmacy, usually the only things open late. Desperate to get dry, I hurried toward it. It was a small police station.

Inside an officer read a newspaper at a counter. Behind him was a large wall map of Paris, not unlike mine hanging in my apartment, which is where I wanted to be more than anything.

I entered, dripping water across the concrete floor. The officer closed his paper and eyed me suspiciously.

"Oui?" he asked. I tried to think of a convincing lie why I was there, but I gave up and told the truth.

"Je suis perdu." I'm lost.

He snorted a laugh, then caught himself. When he realized I was serious he pretended to tie his shoe. When he came up, the veins in his neck were about to burst, his face as red as a summer tomato.

"Un instant, monsieur," he said, biting his lip. He dashed through a door. I heard some low-level chatter in the back room while the puddle under me spread across the floor. Then another officer appeared, wiping the last of a smirk off his face.

"Monsieur?"

"Je suis perdu."

He zipped back through the door, chewing his finger to stifle a laugh. I waited, squishing in my shoes. I looked in a mirror on the wall. I looked like a muskrat that just crawled out of the Seine. Hard to believe where I was just a few hours ago.

They came out together, struggling to look officious. The first one tried to speak, but crumpled on the counter, pounding his fist. The other one at least tried for some decorum, snorting between questions, wanting to know what happened.

I explained I was at a private dinner in the 2nd arrondissement. When I ticked off the landmarks I'd passed on my journey, he traced a finger across the big map. When I told him I lived across town in the 15th, he spun around to see if I was joking. When he saw I wasn't, down he went in a heap with the other cop, clinging to the counter.

It was useless to attempt any sort of professionalism. When they caught their breath, they gestured for me to take a seat by the door. I squish-squished over in my wet shoes. When I sat, my waterlogged wool coat sagged so heavily I could barely breathe. Why in the world did I bring a wool coat to a rainy climate?

Fatigue hit me like a truck. I curled up on the bench, shivering, and closed my eyes.

When I woke up, the cop was behind the counter reading his paper again.

"Ca va, monsieur?," he asked, genuinely concerned.

I sat up and looked around. Every muscle and bone ached. It was still dark outside and still pouring. I shook the cobwebs out of my head.

"Vous avez bien dormi?" I nodded, yes, I slept well, and told him I really wanted to be home.

"Quand vous êtes prêt." Oh, I was ready all right, but how?

A horn honked outside. I struggled to my feet and squished out the door. Outside the other cop stood next to his patrol car, lights twirling. He came around and opened the passenger door. "Montez!" telling me to get in.

I felt like Charlie Brown when Lucy holds the football for him. I looked inside the station.

"Bonsoir, monsieur. Merci!" he said, I guess for the cheap laughs. I looked back at the car. Lucy hadn't pulled the football away yet.

I stepped in and we pulled away. We raced through the wet streets. He asked lots questions about America. He liked the Lakers, Yankees, and Dolphins, wanted to know where to get a good taco if he ever went to the States, and do people really fall into the Grand Canyon, or is that just a myth?

We took a few corners a bit too fast, then dipped into the Pont de l'Alma tunnel. It was odd seeing Paris from a police car. The speed didn't bother me, I was used to Framboise's lead foot, but on a rainy night with lights flashing it was a hoot.

We entered the 15th, I told him my address, and just like that, I was home. He made me promise whenever I got lost, which he was sure I would, I must come to his station. We shook hands. Nicest policeman I ever met. He roared off and I headed upstairs.

After I got into warm pajamas, I studied my wall map, retracing my steps. To this day I have no idea where I went wrong. And I will never forget how those two helped me that night. Or how hard they laughed.

Momma, The Door Nazi

I would have slept all day, but Framboise called, wanting to know what I did last night. I thought of snails, Dominique, and laughing policemen.

"Uh...rien." Nothing.

She invited me for dinner that evening, at her house, with some friends. I could have politely declined. I was exhausted, but she wanted me to meet her two best friends, Hélène and Maylis. She thought we'd all get along. I barely jotted down her address and Métro stop before my head hit the pillow.

That evening, when I stepped off the Métro, I was impressed. Sèvres-Babylone was where I changed Métro lines to go to school. I'd never popped up and looked around. Wow. I found the address and stood outside an imposing 17th century apartment building. I found Framboise's name and buzzed it.

"Oui?" snapped a take-no-prisoners female voice. I was expecting to hear Framboise's lilting giggle, not a drill sergeant.

"I...I...I..." The security buzzer exploded.

BUZZZZZZZZZZZZZZZZZZZZZZZZZZZZZZZZ.
It sounded like a hornet swarm. It rattled the hinges, it was so loud. I stepped into the small courtyard and slammed the gate.

BUZZZZZZZZZZZZZZZZZZZZZZZZZZZZZZZZ.
It wouldn't stop. I shook the gate, hoping it was just stuck. How long do they think it takes someone to step through a gate? It droned on for more than a minute.

BUZZZZZZZZZZZZZZZZZZZZZZZZZZZZZZZZ.
I looked up at the open windows. Not to speak, I was worried someone might hurl a skillet at me.

BUZZZZZZZZZZZZZZZZZZZZZZZZZZZZZZZZ...
Silence.

Last night I walked ten miles easier than these ten feet. I hopped up three steps to the door of the building. I pressed the button.

"Oh, no..."

BUZZZZZZZZZZZZZZZZZZZZZZZZZZZZZZZZ.
I stepped into the foyer and shut the door behind me. With a three-story ceiling, tile floors, and concrete walls, the noise echoed like a giant shower stall. I sat at the foot of a winding staircase. I plugged my ears and closed my eyes.

When I opened them, there was a pair of shoes standing next to me. I looked up. They belonged to a pretty girl with brown hair and a welcoming smile. I was relieved that she was casually dressed in jeans and sweater, since I didn't know what was appropriate attire for a dinner party.

She yelled over the din. I yelled back, but we couldn't hear each other. At this rate, we'd be deaf and hoarse before we'd properly met. She bellowed up the stairway in a most unfeminine way, "Momma!"

BUZZZZZZZZZZZZZZZZZZZZZZZZZZZZZZZZ.
"MOMMA!"
BUZZZZZZZZZZZZZZ...BUZZZZZZZZZZ...B-B-B-B-B-B. Silence.

We took a breath and introduced ourselves. She was Hélène. We chatted a bit. She knew various tidbits of my short life in Paris. I knew she was one-half of Framboise's best-friend duo. They'd all met in college and had been inseparable ever since.

A shadow appeared on the landing. A woman studied us with a motherly glare. She descended the stairway, her back ramrod straight. Each foot landed perfectly centered on each step. No wasted motion.

Worse, she was overdressed in a knee-length business suit and hose. Her hair was pulled back, not a strand out of place, accentuating her dark, penetrating eyes. I was hoping she was a stranger on her way to somewhere else, but she stopped on the step above us, staring me down.

"Maylis," she said, simple as that. Ah, the Door Nazi.

She extended her hand. I took it. She yanked it hard one time in the French fashion. Almost separated my shoulder. As imposing as she looked on the landing, when she joined us, she was quite petite. Her demeanor elevated her.

While chatting with Hélène, it was effortless. But with Momma, I snapped to attention and answered her like a school boy.

I didn't mind her direct questions because I could understand her. Meeting strangers is tense, not knowing if you will understand them. These two I did. Hélène, like everyone, affectionately called her "Momma."

Momma was their age, early twenties, but seemed older. She told me she was certain I had no problem entering the building because she pressed the button "slightly" longer than usual. Hélène smiled at me behind her back as Momma turned and climbed the stairs.

"Venez," Momma ordered, over her shoulder, like a mother to her children. Come. And we did. Up the stairs and into Framboise's apartment. Well, her parents' apartment. They were gone for the weekend.

This was nothing like Ann's cramped quarters at Saint-Michel. This one ran the entire length of the building. We walked on creaky wood floors that led into a large foyer, that led into the large dining room.

There were people sitting at the large table. Framboise and Hélène introduced me around. They were all nice, and offered me a splash of scotch. I don't drink scotch, but when meeting a roomful of strangers, you need all the help you can get.

We went into the kitchen, which was a beehive of activity. Momma was supervising several women preparing the dinner. One look and I understood I wasn't wanted. The French are terrified of Americans in their kitchens, as if we're going to sprinkle poison on the food, or worse, want to help.

The apartment had high ceilings and no hallways, just doorways leading to more rooms, making it seem even larger than it was. There was a long, well-worn living room with mismatched furniture and faded pillows.

After a series of bedrooms, we reached a corner sitting area with a TV and stacks of videos. A few people were watching *Les Bronzés Font du Ski*, a timeless, nonsensical comedy, a French *Caddyshack*. They gestured me to join them, but Framboise pulled me through another set of doors.

The apartment was "L" shaped. At the end was a suite of rooms with its own bathroom and sitting room. She offered it to me anytime I wanted to return to Paris.

Momma's voice boomed all the way from the kitchen. Framboise and Hélène hurried back giggling, imitating Momma. I was overwhelmed at my good fortune to meet such nice people.

****

We had a terrific dinner. I couldn't keep up with their questions, but the girls jumped in and finished my sentences, mostly Framboise because she knew me best.

As the evening wore on, I realized I was on the other side of the party equation. I would have to find my way home without the Métro. After dinner we cleaned up the French way, which is to dump everything in the sink and leave it until next week.

Then Framboise grabbed her car keys and coat. Hélène pushed me out the door, and the three of us walked down to the stairs to the foyer. BUZZZZZZZZZZZZZZ.

We stepped into the courtyard, buzzer blaring. Framboise rattled a rusty key into a splintered door and kicked it viciously until it gave up and scraped open. We climbed into her car and backed into the street. Hélène rolled the window down.

BUZZZZZZZZZZZZZZZZZZZZZZZZZZZZZZZZZZ. A little high from the scotch, I cursed from the back seat, badly, and I knew it. That's all it took. We all grabbed our sides, and in the middle of the street we started silent, side-splitting, laughter. We couldn't get a breath.

BUZZZZZZZZZZZZZZZZZZZZZZZZZZZZZZZZZZZ.

Framboise was laughing so hard she couldn't push the clutch in, so she grinded it into gear. The car lurched and

swerved down the street. We could still hear the buzzer as we rounded the turn at the end of the block.
BUZZZZZZZZZZZZZZZZZZZZZZZZZZZZZZZ…

Ghost Stories in Normandy

In late fall, Framboise invited me to her family's vacation home in tiny Jullouville on the Normandy coast with some friends. I had to ride the train out, as most of them would already be there, opening up the place.

Framboise picked me up at the station. When we pulled up to the house, there was a young man standing in the doorway, as if he owned the place.

"That's Augustin," Framboise said. His sad eyes and slow manner hid a dry, biting wit which he never failed to use.

The house was two-story, with plenty of room for friends to hang out, comfy and warm. In the kitchen Momma was giving Hélène a lesson in potato slicing. Hélène looked at me like, *she thinks I don't know how to slice potatoes?*

Momma, now Potato Nazi.

One day we went to Mont Saint-Michel, the island monastery a kilometer off the coast. No matter how many pictures you've seen of it, nothing compares to seeing it up close. Sitting atop a huge rock, it's an island, until the tide recedes and you can drive or walk out to it.

We walked its narrow paths up to the church at the top. On the way down, we ate galettes, buckwheat crêpes. It was a beautiful, clear day, and it was great to be surrounded by the ocean and good friends.

You can't eat galettes without drinking the local cider, so it only took a glass for Framboise to bring up the dreaded crêpe Grand Marnier story for those who hadn't heard it.

She plowed in, even remembering the woman in the red dress who stopped traffic. When she finished, Augustin asked me to give it a try. I sloshed a mouthful of cider for some confidence.

"Crêpe Grarn...Marn yarn yer ray."

Hélène covered her face with a napkin. Momma was horrified, as if I'd lifted my leg on a Rodin. Augustin scratched his chin, searching for the right word. "Pathétique." Luckily the tide was creeping in, so we had to leave or be stranded and have to pay for overpriced rooms.

Another day we visited Omaha Beach, and the town of Caen, about thirty times. I liked seeing the French struggle with French road signs. We had stopped in Caen for lunch, but couldn't leave, endlessly looping around and passing the same shops and, embarrassingly, the same people. We must have looked ridiculous, Framboise and Hélène laughing and cursing up front, Momma in the back with the map, Augustin and I keeping out of it.

Something else happened. I spoke French. Away from the rigors of the classroom, and in the cozy confines of friends, my brain loosened up. I made mistakes, sure. Augustin pointed out every one. But he did it in such a funny way with his vulgar sense of humor, all you could do was laugh.

We were lost on a back road, things were getting tense with the girls. Sensing it, Augustin tossed off a horribly off-color joke about a nun and a blind, one-legged platypus. Hélène laughed so hard she lost control and drove us into a ditch. She and Framboise held their stomachs and howled. Even normally stoic Momma gave in, face red as a beet. I didn't care how we'd get the car out, I was happy I understood the joke. Augustin, of course, never cracked a smile.

Another day we joined up with some other of their friends and spent the day at the beach. We swam in the cold water. Well, they swam; I got in up to my ankles before I ran out screaming like a girl. I can barely get in the water in southern California; no way could I get in the frigid English Channel.

At sunset we grilled fish in a makeshift pit in the sand and drank wine. When it got dark, Augustin told a story about a dysfunctional ghost family who were so fat they couldn't fly. Ghost Dad wanted to haunt a house around the corner, but they only got as far as next door before they were bickering with each other.

Ghost Mom wanted to finish some knitting, and the ghost kids wanted to be at the mall with their friends. Ghost Dad brought a copy of *Haunting For Dummies*, but no one could read. They were so fat they couldn't get in the front door, so they knocked it down and went straight to the kitchen and ended up in a food fight.

I whispered to Framboise, "How long does this go on?"

"Une heure, minimum."

"An hour!"

Augustin glared at me as if I'd interrupted a private reading of the Dead Sea Scrolls. There was nothing to do but pour more wine and listen to his stupid, fat ghost story. A half-hour into it, I rolled over to sleep. The last thing I remembered was Mom and Dad ghost in the master bedroom trying on clothes.

The next morning I felt a strange presence in my room. I opened one eye. Augustin was sitting in a chair staring at me. Without even a "bonjour" he picked up the story right where I had fallen asleep in the sand, with the two kid ghosts fighting over a pair of Doc Martins.

I rode the train back to Paris thinking of what fun I had: crashing into a ditch, galettes at Mont Saint-Michel, a one-legged platypus, and ghosts trying on clothes.

Costume Party

In the winter, I was invited for the weekend to a costume party at Hélène's family's home in Gommegnies, 150 miles north of Paris near the Belgian border. Like snails, I don't do costumes, and I wasn't sure how they'd take it. Framboise and Momma went up early to help Hélène and her family with preparations, so I took the train. Momma picked me up at the station.

It was a stone country home with creaky floors and a large fireplace. It was over 100 years old, built like a fortress, and looked like there had not been one bit of upkeep over the years. In the States, if you neglect a house for a hundred years, it would collapse; but this one looked like it could last another five hundred.

Momma and Hélène showed me around and re-introduced me to their friends from the party months before, and some new ones.

Guests were scattered all over the grounds, and in groups in the large rooms, but no Framboise. She was putting the final touches on her costume. This, I had to see.

They gave me a tour of the house, ending in the kitchen where I met Hélène's family. And then Framboise entered in blue jeans, T-shirt, and a straw hat. She waited for someone to guess who she was. The only thing I came up with was James Dean in a barbershop quartet.

She turned slowly, but it was still blue jeans, T-shirt, and that hat. No one could come up with anything, so she stomped off. Great way to start the weekend.

That afternoon I listened to all sorts of stories. I struggled with the slang, which isn't taught in language school, but I got most of it. Someone asked me about Thanksgiving. The French are fascinated with it. Like most Americans, I couldn't tie it all together with Pilgrims and Indians, with turkey and cranberries. None of which they ate all those years ago, I think.

I thought I remembered the word for turkey, dinde-dinde. But every time I used it people cocked their heads like confused dogs. But I blundered on, fearing if I stopped I'd lose my train of thought. After the fifth dinde-dinde, I turned to Framboise to make sure it was the right word. She shrugged, still miffed I couldn't guess her costume.

That night she told me the word was dinde, not the double dinde-dinde. I had confused it with dindon, another word for turkey, and had come up with the nonsensical dinde-dinde. I asked her why she didn't correct me, instead of letting me go on like a fool. She said she would have, if I had guessed her costume.

In bed, I stared at the ceiling, thinking what a fool I must have sounded like. "In America we eat turkey-turkey. We call it turkey-turkey day. While the turkey-turkey is in the oven we make gravy from turkey-turkey drippings." My face burned in the dark and I wondered if I'd ever get the hang of the language.

The next morning, breakfast was outside on the big side lawn, self-serve French style. Cases of milk cartons and juice were torn open next to a picnic table stacked with bowls, instant coffee, an electric kettle, and various hot and cold cereals. And some wondrous soul had made a run to the local *patissière*.

Guests staggered across the lawn like the walking dead, puffy-eyed, toward the food. Most were in pajamas, some were still in their costumes. Maybe a little too much wine and fun.

Momma, a non-drinker (though we try...), was dressed perfectly, alert, and ready for door monitor duty, or potato slicing.

I had just poured coffee when one of the guys who had listened patiently to my dinde-dinde speech approached.

"You want a cup-cup?," he asked

"Excuse me?" My brain was still a bit fuzzy.

"For your coffee-coffee. The milk-milk is over there, next to the bread-bread, on the table-table." I can blush in the dark, or in bright sunlight. Makes no difference to me.

Framboise, still in her costume, was sipping her coffee-coffee on a bench, still smoldering from last night. I suspected she had put him up to this. I walked over, and stared long and hard at her costume. If I could guess correctly, we could call a truce. Maybe.

"James Dean?" No reaction. "Wyatt Earp?" She rolled her eyes at the heavens. "I give up."

"Groucho Marx," she snapped.

"Groucho Marx? In a straw hat and blue jeans?"

She stormed off and got into a heated discussion with some others. Someone corrected her. She argued back, then listened as the others jumped all over her. She came back, tail between her legs. It killed her to admit she was wrong.

"Charlie Chaplin. I didn't have a cane." As if the cane was the problem. I figured that was as much of an apology as I'd get. Another guy came up to me.

"I was in America last year," he said.

"Yeah?" I said, waiting for the punch line.

He had gone to a baseball game, of which he understood nothing. As he put it, a man in the middle does all the work while one squats, and the other seven stand around scratching and pulling at themselves. Once an hour the ball goes somewhere, and one of the lazy players throws it back to the man in the middle doing all the work. Couldn't argue with that, and I was relieved he didn't ask me to explain the infield fly rule.

During the game, a man handed him a wad of cash and told him to pass it down. As he's telling this, a crowd gathers. Soon, hot dogs, sodas, peanuts, and change come the other way. He passed it to the man next to him, who hands him ten dollars. He passes it down. The man taps him on the shoulder. His two little kids in baseball caps, mustard smeared all over their face, wave and holler 'Thank you!'

"C'est fantastique! Nobody steals!" He couldn't believe the honesty and cooperation at an American sporting event. He explained to the crowd in French. They were shocked.

A woman asked me if this was rare. I told her no, we did it all the time.

"And no one takes the money?" she asked.

"Why would we take their money?" I asked.

"That would never happen in France," she said. "If a stranger hands me money, it goes in my pocket." Everyone nodded in agreement. "You Americans are crazy!" They all nodded again. Then we all laughed, but they were impressed. And no one brought up dinde-dinde again.

RIDING THE RAILS

When I returned to Paris, most of the tourists had left. It was time for my much-needed trip, on the advice of the teacher at the party. I shut off the water heater, informed my concierge I'd be gone for a while, and then headed off to Gare de Lyon to validate my rail pass.

It was liberating to stare out the window at the French countryside. All those people living in their quaint houses, and not one of them cared I couldn't remember the imperfect tense.

First up, Strasbourg on the French and German border. Captured and liberated so many times between the two countries, everything is a mixture. The food, language, architecture--you're not quite sure where you are. Boulangeries have croissants and strudel. Stores sell French wine and cheese with German names. Bottom line, it's all great.

For the first time in a long time I felt useful. I was having dinner in a small bistro just off the main cathedral square. An American couple was struggling with the menu at the next table and was looking around for help. I went over and struck up a conversation.

They were on their honeymoon. I helped them order and they asked me to sit. They told me about meeting in college, their engagement, and how they wanted to travel for their honeymoon. They poured me some wine and I left them alone to enjoy their dinner. It's nice to see young love. It gives you hope.

The next day, I got up early and hopped on a train. I stepped off in fairyland Lucerne. The people spoke softly as they strolled through the train station. Lake Lucerne shimmers emerald green against the Alps. With my trusted guidebook under my arm, I checked into a small, but not cheap, hotel.

The next morning, I climbed aboard a cruise around Lake Lucerne. It stops at small-town harbors, and you can come and go as you please. There was something about the little town of Vitznau that prompted me to get off and wander.

I followed some people onto Rigi-Kulm, a rack railway designed to haul passengers up steep Mount Rigi. The toothed middle rail makes a sturdy but jerky ride. We chugged slowly and steeply up the mountain. It was a white-knuckler. I didn't dare look behind me.

We stopped at the top of Mount Rigi in front of a lodge with picnic tables on a wide lawn. There must have been a hundred people drinking beer from enormous mugs. Most of the men, and sadly only a few of the women, had their shirts off. Beer all around on a brisk sunny morning. My kind of people. My kind of place. To top it off, a Saint Bernard was sunning himself on the sloped roof, keeping an eye on everyone.

I wandered the steep grassy slopes, with the Alps all around me. As I looked at the magnificent peaks I wondered, how the hell do I get down?

Out of nowhere, a young girl approached to admire the views. She seemed as lost as me. Her name was Katie, with a smile as bright as the sun reflecting off the snow peaks. We decided to have lunch together. We grabbed a spot at the picnic tables and had lunch with the Saint Bernard looking over our shoulders.

Katie was from Zurich, the youngest of eleven children, with a loving mother and a hateful father. She was getting away for a bit, and didn't want to discuss it any more than that. We strolled around a while and after a few beers, she decided we should hike down the mountain. She was serious. She did it all the time; we just had to find the switchbacks.

About halfway down, the trail leveled out into a small village. We bought some chocolate and shared it as we strolled around. The intense sun melted it all over our hands and faces. We looked like two kids who raided the cookie jar. Katie washed up in a stream and used my shirt as a towel, which she thought was hilarious. I decided I would leave my chocolate on. Katie headed down the trail and reminded me that bears can smell chocolate a kilometer away. I quickly washed up and ran to catch up.

Back in Lucerne, Katie took me to the Lion Monument, a gorgeous sculpture, chiseled into the side of a mountain. It's about thirty feet long and twenty feet high. The lion is wounded, impaled by a spear. He's protecting a French fleur-de-lis shield that represents the Swiss guards killed during the French Revolution. At least that's what my guidebook said.

Katie said the lion was Switzerland's symbol of independence in 1291 when farmers banded together to protect their crops from enemies. The inscription reads: "To the loyalty and bravery of the Swiss," so maybe it's both. Mark Twain felt it was the most mournful and moving piece of stone in the world. I'll side with Katie and Mr. Twain on that one.

We walked the covered bridge that crossed the lake, with its engraved cross beams chronicling Lucerne's history, and ended up at a lakeside café. I shared some of my pretzel with the swans and ducks pecking at my ankles.

As the sun got low, Katie had to catch a train back to Zurich. I walked her to the station. She promised to come visit me in Paris. I waved until her train disappeared out of the station, then wandered the lake's edge looking for another beer. Or two. I liked the Swiss. I wanted to come back.

Two Gentlemen From Verona

The next morning, I lingered at a café in the station, then caught a train to Goeshenen for a quick change to Verona.

On the train two elderly women across from me were deep in discussion. One was speaking Italian, the other Spanish. They spoke slowly so they could be understood. They asked me to join in.

I dusted off my high school Spanish, and before long Clara invited me to dinner at her home in Padua, and I helped the Spaniard catch her transfer to Trento.

Clara knew English and French, so of course she spoke French. She impressed me with her knowledge of Renaissance art, and why Giotto's contributions in his Capella Scrovegni were so important in her beloved Padua. When I stepped off the train in Verona, I had her address, phone number and a date for a walking tour of Padua, provided I could keep up with her, she chided.

I looked at a row of public buses lined up outside the station. I had no idea which one to take, so I chatted up two girls with backpacks. They were headed to the youth hostel, so I followed them onto bus #1.

In a few minutes we were passing Piazza Brà and a perfectly preserved Roman coliseum in the center of town. We crossed the river Adige. We got off and I followed them up a hill and into a fifteenth century palazzo, the popular Verona youth hostel.

They were Kate and Tracy from Scotland, and they were meeting up with two other friends, Debbie and Nancy, and were kind enough to show me the ropes.

One minute I was lost in Verona, the next I'm sitting on ancient steps with a belly full of wine and pasta. Someone suggested we go downtown, and before long, we were back on bus #1 rumbling into town.

The coliseum in Verona is smaller than its Roman counterpart, but perfectly preserved. Cafés ring around it, bustling with activity. We watched the well-dressed Veronese strolling around it, arm in arm.

I suggested we do the same, ice cream and a stroll. Kate corrected me. It was *gelato* and a *passeggiata*. Women from every corner of the globe never miss an opportunity to correct me.

After a few *passeggiate* around the coliseum, we window shopped down some narrow streets before it was time to head back to our own private palazzo before lights out.

The sleeping arrangements were army-barracks style beds, against opposite walls, and an aisle down the middle. The high-ceilinged room buzzed with backpackers swapping information and studying maps.

I was eavesdropping on a conversation when a pasty-faced man with slicked back hair passed by, twirling a pair of wet socks like airplane propellers. They were stretched out like dancer's tights, had to be three-feet long. He looked like Dracula piloting a DC-10.

His bony knees jutted out of a poorly tied bathrobe. If he hit a crosswind, you'd see his landing gear. He throttled back, applied right rudder, and taxied up to me. Me, one of a hundred men in the room.

"I'm Lazslo from Budapest!" he bellowed.

You couldn't clear the room faster with a scared skunk. Lazslo was well-known in backpacking circles, and no one wanted any part of the mad Hungarian. Everyone faked yawning and saying "Good night" in ten languages.

"Know what I'm doing?" he asked me. I really didn't care. "I'm drying my socks!" He revved them up to 2800 RPM, taxied over to his bed, and shut down both engines. He slid his socks up to his bombay doors, what a sight that was, and fell asleep instantly.

A backpacker next to me witnessed the whole thing.

"Bit of a dink, wouldn't you say?" he asked, in a Yorkshire drawl.

"I'll say," I answered.

"You'll say what?" he asked, confused.

"That he's a dink," I said, equally confused.

"Actually, I said, he's a bit of a dink. That's different."

"How so?"

"How so, what? Good God, you haven't made a lick of sense! Where you from, mate?" When I told him he replied "I knew there was something off about you." And that's how I met Mark from England.

We became fast friends. The next morning we rode bus #1 into town and had a coffee and pastry, then wandered around the open market in Piazza Brà. Mark headed off to find a pub, pointing out it was already 10:00 am. We agreed to hook up later at the entrance to the Coliseum.

I was picking out some fruit when I noticed a girl from the youth hostel. She had orange hair, freckles, and green eyes. Her name was Katrina. We chatted a bit, and I told her that my ancestors came from Ireland and that I'd like to someday visit the Emerald Isle.

But she was Belgian, on her way to hike the Lake District before returning to Brussels to finish medical school to be a surgeon. Great, then she could remove my foot from my mouth.

I made an obscure reference to Flanders because I wasn't sure what or where it was. She snapped back she was Walloon, and spoke French. Flemish was the language of their enemies. It was a tight fit, but I got the other foot in.

She was lugging a huge backpack but insisted on spending a few hours wandering Verona before catching her bus. She spoke slow, deliberate French for me. I was surprised that I understood her, and that I could speak a little. We exchanged addresses and she promised to visit Paris. Not me, Paris.

This willingness to invite strangers to my apartment was new to me. If we spoke on the street for an hour you'd be lucky to learn my name, but here I was as welcoming as a doorman at the Waldorf.

I walked her to her waiting bus. She hopped on and waved good-bye. I was proud of myself. We spent three hours together, and after my awkward hello, I never spoke another word of English. That teacher at the party was winning me over.

I met up with Mark at the coliseum. He'd found a pub, or two, judging from his eyes. We climbed to the top and looked out over the olive groves that held the history of Romeo and Juliet.

We watched people strolling below like ants. Mark couldn't find anything decent to hurl at them, so at the top of his lungs, he recited Monty Python's, "What Have the Romans Ever Done For Us?" scene from *Life of Brian*, listing Rome's staggering contributions to modern society. But he was drawing a crowd, mostly Security. It was time to leave.

We caught the bus back to the youth hostel. I had been away only three days from Paris, but it seemed like a year. At the steps of the hostel, an irrational feeling came over me that I might never see my apartment again. Mark said to forget Paris, and that if we didn't hurry up, we might not see dinner.

The next morning we took a day trip to Venice. Mark understood what I was doing, living in Paris, and was insanely jealous. He was a devout traveler, but had to wedge his trips in between his job's demands.

We walked all over Venice, not by choice; we were hopelessly lost. It seemed no matter which way we turned, we either hit a dead end, or water, or both. Before we knew it, we were rushing back to the station to catch the last train back to Verona. He invited himself to Paris, and insisted I come to England.

The next day we said good-bye at breakfast. He would head north to go home after breakfast. I caught a train south to Bologna to visit Silvia.

Silvia, Rita, and a Flat Tire

I hadn't seen Silvia since I tossed her luggage onto her departing train. She had booked me a room in a B&B, so I grabbed a taxi at the station, and stopped in a residential neighborhood.

I knocked on the door. A scowling matronly woman opened it. She was dressed like an old Italian photograph, in a heavy floor-length skirt, grey blouse, and sweater. She looked like a nun, which made me think of Augustin's one-legged platypus joke. I still can't believe he told it in front of three women.

Signora eyed me suspiciously from behind a torn screen. With a grunt, she let me into her house. I followed her down a long hallway, and still couldn't get the platypus out of my mind. We passed several rooms that looked like they hadn't been remodeled in a hundred years.

Signora led me to tiny room #3, containing two single beds. I found the bathroom, which looked like it missed the renovation a hundred years ago. I didn't see how, but I hoped I wouldn't have to use it. Mark had worn me out, so I stretched out on a bed and fell asleep.

I awoke to the aroma of heavenly tomato sauce simmering. I hopped out of bed and headed to Signora's kitchen. She was stirring sauce on the stove, looking over her shoulder at me, as if protecting it. I rubbed my tummy in anticipation as I left, letting her know I couldn't wait until dinner. She spat something under her breath, shaking her head.

I met up with Silvia at San Pietro church. I suggested we speak English. She ignored me and spoke French. The Italians share some French traits. We strolled down Bologna's arcaded sidewalks. I told her about my snail dinner and other mishaps with the language. She asked me if I thought I'd ever get the hang of French.

"No," I replied, without hesitation. She agreed.

We stopped to window shop. While Silvia admired the stylish clothes, two Italian men studied us, mumbling to each other. It wasn't hard to figure out what they were thinking; how does that guy get to spend time with one of our beautiful Bolognese? Silvia ignored them and kept looking at the clothes in the window.

After they left, I asked her what they were saying.

"I don't know, they were speaking dialect from another region."

Not that long ago, before Italy was Italy, people spoke a dialect unique to their region, Emilia-Romagna, Tuscany, Veneto, etc. It wasn't until the 1920s, with the introduction of the radio that Italians heard a language other than what they spoke locally.

With television in the 1950s, linguistic unification really took off, establishing Florentine Italian as the standard. Regional pride has kept dialects alive, and they will use them when they don't want to be understood, like when ogling a Bolognese beauty.

As I've said before, I'm genetically inclined to mistakes, and I made another one. I suggested a day trip to Florence. Silvia bristled.

"Why go *there* when there is so much to see *here*?" she fumed. Italians are still provincial, never understanding why you'd want to be any place except *their* region. I waited for the steam from her ears to clear. We compromised on Urbino in the Marche region.

Tomorrow would be a long day, so we cut the evening short. Besides, I had a hot meal waiting for me at my B&B. We would meet in the piazza at 9:00 am.

I knocked on Signora's door. She glared at me through the torn screen. "Camera!" she barked. "Camera!" I never thought of her as a shutterbug, but I handed her my camera. She shoved it back and yelled again. There went my finger again, pointing to the sky, then I looked it up in my dictionary.

Camera. Room. Oh.

I held up three fingers. She let me in. The aroma of the sauce was so divine I headed straight to the kitchen and sat at the table. I fluffed a napkin into my lap and waited. She stared at me, wondering what to do with me, then made a telephone call. Maybe inviting some friends?

She ladled sauce over a bowl of bowties and pulled up a stool at the sink. A bit rude, I thought. I figured it was serve yourself, so I did. She watched me take a bite. I gave her a "thumbs up."

Just then, someone stormed in the front door and marched down the hallway. A middle-aged man in a suit burst in, furious.

"Get out of my mother's kitchen! You think this is a Bed & Breakfast?" Actually, I did. He came at me, but I was already up and out the door. I was two blocks away before I realized I still had my napkin in my collar.

I found a small restaurant, ordered the special with a carafe of wine, and stayed until they kicked me out. When I returned, I tiptoed down the hall and closed my bedroom door.

The next morning I put on my best clothes. I was going to spend the day traveling with Silvia across the Po Valley to historic Urbino, home of Renaissance master Raphael. But first I had to get away from the jerk who sat across from me at breakfast. They always find me, like flies to carrion.

He had blown in during the night, crashing around in the dark. I'm not a doctor, but it's safe to say his brain wasn't connected to anything. When he plopped down across from me, he reached across and took a gulp of my coffee. "Just 'til mine gets here," he said.

After a long gulp of my water, he wiped his mouth on his sleeve and went into a diatribe on American women. He had decided to come to Italy to meet, as he put it, "some Guatemalonian women from South America."

I found him wildly entertaining. When I asked why he was in Italy and not Guatemala, he wagged his finger at me and answered, "Jews should stay in Egypt, with the Mormons." I think he meant Muslims, but he was on a roll, and who was I to stop him?

By the time we finished breakfast, I figured this nut would be a million laughs, crammed in a car with short-tempered Silvia. When I invited him, he slid his chair back, belched, and said "Life is experience, but if you own something, you're screwed." I took it as a no.

I walked under the arcades to San Pietro. It was a beautiful autumn day. For once I could sit back and let someone else do all the work, until I rounded a corner onto the piazza, and saw Silvia's car with a flat tire. Right rear.

In France if you have a flat tire no one helps. It's your problem, not theirs. In Italy, they pour out of neighboring towns to watch. Not help. Watch. You would have thought the Pope was in town, everyone in their Sunday best, crowded around a flat tire. Church could wait.

The tire wasn't just flat, it was shredded to the rim. I'd have to change it, in my slacks and white shirt. I had to ask.

"Silvia, how long have you been driving on the rim?"

"A week."

"Why didn't you get it changed before?"

"I knew you were coming."

Then a young lady poked her head out the back seat window waving a road map, as if we were holding her up. Rita, Silvia's friend. An Italian Momma. I opened the trunk and pulled out a crowbar, jack, and a flat spare.

When I mentioned this to Silvia, she pointed out, "Flat, but not shredded."

The crowd squeezed in, while I rolled up my sleeves and jacked the car up, with Rita still inside, circling points of interest on her map. While loosening the lug nuts, a man leaned in so close I could tell his brand of coffee. Every time I twisted, my elbow bumped his chin. After the tenth bump I said, "Would you please move back?" He nodded, and inched closer.

I removed the shredded tire, which got a round of applause. But the crowd was packed in so tightly there was no place to put it. Rita leaned out the window and barked an order. The crowd backed off just enough for me to drop it, then encroached even closer, I guess for the main event.

I put on the flat spare, and tightened the lug nuts, bumping Coffee Breath with every twist. In Italy, on or off, lugs nuts are fascinating. I lowered the car onto the flat tire, and threw the tools in the trunk. Everyone broke out in applause.

Silvia fired up her car. She revved the engine and honked the horn, but no one moved, too busy talking about The Changing of the Tire. Rita leaned out her window and barked. The crowd parted and let us through.

We headed, I thought, to a gas station to fill the tire. But Silvia aimed the car onto the highway and let 'er rip. I looked at Silvia, then Rita in the backseat, window down, map slapping her face.

"Silvia, aren't we going to get air in the tire?"

"On Sunday? In Italy?" Like I was an idiot.

We stopped at a friend's house. He came out and handed me a rusty bicycle pump. I thought it was a joke. I twisted the nozzle on and started pumping. In one minute I was wringing wet, in two I thought I'd pass out.

It took over an hour, with Silvia and her friend sitting under a tree. Rita never got out of the car. She watched me, hanging her head out the window like a dog. When I stood up I was so lightheaded I had to hold onto the car.

We buzzed through the Emilia-Romangna countryside. We had lunch on the Adriatic coast town of Gabicce Mare, then up to the magnificent hill town of Urbino. With me, Rita, and Silvia, the population that day was 3. We strolled the streets and never saw a soul. When we spoke on the brick streets, our voices echoed off the buildings.

Rita, now buried in her guidebook, rattled off the sights, Palazzo Ducale and its basilica, the frescoes of San Dominico. It would have been great to see them, but Urbino was locked up tighter than Fort Knox. As we toured its perimeter, Rita ticked off more sites we wouldn't see. "If this building on the left were open, we would see its priceless frescoes. If that building over there were open, we would see Raphael's home..."

I asked Silvia if she knew everything would be closed. "Of course, it's Sunday," she replied. Again, like I'm an idiot.

After that, there was nothing to do but drive all day, so we talked. Silvia told Rita about our terrific summer in Paris, and all our mishaps. Rita laughed until her sides ached, and wished she could have been there. Then Silvia asked about my apartment. Something stabbed at my heart. I missed Paris. Silvia sensed it.

"Ne t'inquiètes pas," Silvia said. "Paris sera là quand tu reviens." Don't worry, Paris will be there when you return.

Maybe.

The next morning I was on a train to Padua to take Clara up on her invitation to visit her town. I was to meet her at Piazzale Borscetti at noon. And there she was, on time and itching to show me around town before taking me home for lunch. She was a robust eighty years young, and chided me for not coming next weekend to join her skiing in the Alps.

There is nothing like seeing someone's city through their eyes. She took me to Basilica San Francisco where she was married, had coffee in the caffé where they celebrated, visited her grammar school, and ate desserts at a restaurant too rich for my budget.

Clara went home to prepare dinner. I spent the rest of the day at tiny Capella Scrovegni, the birthplace of Italian Renaissance art, and admired Giotto's masterpieces. Exhausted, I returned to Clara's home.

Helping Clara cook was her daughter Carla, a French professor. So we spoke French. I think I did okay, but the bottle of Barolo helped. It always does.

The next day, the three of us rode bicycles all over Padua. There were supposed to be five of us, with Carla's friends, Anna-Lise and Aldo joining us. But their bikes had flats so they couldn't come. Aldo wanted to fill me up with Prosecco, but he had to help an uncle with a broken refrigerator. He would join up with us later, if he could get his cousin's lawnmower started. My head was spinning.

Clara was ready to fill out adoption papers on me. Living in Italy would be wonderful. Aldo and I could sell tire patches. Everyone seemed to need them.

After dinner Clara packed a prosciutto and provolone sandwich, and fruit for my trip. I stuffed it in my rucksack, but couldn't zip it all the way. Then she reserved a couchette for me on the night train to Germany.

I was looking forward to the trip. I hadn't taken a night train in years, and I liked the idea of falling asleep in Padua and waking up in Ulm, Germany, Didi's hometown.

Clara hugged me like I was one of her own. Carla drove me to the station and made sure the ticketing was right. You never know. I climbed aboard and waved goodbye from my top bunk.

Deep into the night, the gentle sway of the train lulled me to sleep. Then the door opened and a mangy German Shepherd leaped up and knocked the wind out of me. He clawed my chest until he could look out the window.

He was fascinated with the lights, which were flying past at 100 miles an hour, and he barked at every one. When he tired of that, he plopped down on my chest, jammed his snout into my armpit, and fell asleep.

His owner lit a cigarette under the No Smoking sign. Then he turned on the overhead light and read the paper. In Italy, as in Paris, you choose your battles.

He wasn't a bad dog, but he stunk to high heaven. I squirmed and rolled all night, but he never got the hint I didn't want him on top of me.

When I woke up, I was pushed against the wall and the dog was asleep on my pillow, snout still stuffed under my arm. And he had eaten the sandwich Clara made for me. And the plastic bag it was in. That should be interesting later in the day.

The dog had a foul-smelling ointment on his coat, and now it was on me. The train rolled to a stop in Ulm's train station. The dog got excited, and ran up and down me before leaping off the bunk. Didi knocked on the window and waved. Stinky barked back. A lot.

SCHEIBE!

It was great to see Didi again. He had already been to the fleischmarkt for an impressive array of sausages, würst, and breads. Taking nothing away from the charcuteries of France and Italy, German delicatessens are second to none.

The day was set, a walking tour of Ulm, a picnic on the Danube with his friend Jörg, then to München to meet Peter and his girlfriend, Amel.

Ulm is a small, beautiful town, birthplace of Albert Einstein. Anchoring the center square is the Ulmer Münster, with the highest church spire in the world at 530 feet. How high is that? I climbed the 765 steps and saw the snow-capped Alps 100 miles away. Careful, it's windy up there and not for the queasy.

We picnicked on the grassy banks of the Danube as swans swirled past in the slow current. Before we headed out to Munich, we stopped by Didi's house for me to meet his father, who we called Papa. Papa was remodeling, and Didi asked me to help Papa move a table to the basement. Sure, why not?

Papa and I spoke exactly zero words of each other's language, but we were only moving a table to the basement, for cryin' out loud. He grabbed the front and I grabbed the back. He flipped on the light and backed down the narrow stairway to the basement. The table jostled a bit.

"Ab."

"What?" I asked.

"Ab! Ab!"

Sounded like "up" to me, so I lifted my end. Cursing bubbled up from below.

"Scheiße!" That word I knew. "Shit." Pronounced SHY-zeh. I guess the table wasn't high enough, so I raised my end until it smashed the light bulb on the ceiling. The stairwell went dark as shards of glass slid down the table and onto his head.

"Scheiße!" There was that word again.

The more he yelled "Ab!" the more I lifted, banging the table against the ceiling.

"Didi! Di-di!" he yelled.

Didi skidded around the corner and saw me holding the table over my head. He burst out laughing. He turned on a light at the bottom of the stairwell. Papa was on the ground, pinned against the wall with the table on his chest. Shards of glass were caught in his hair. And I did it all by myself.

Between laughs, Didi asked if he was okay. "Ya, ya, scheiße." He was fine. Didi slithered down the stairwell, lowered the table, and helped Papa to his feet.

They carried the table around the corner. I could hear Papa cursing and Didi laughing as they shoved the table into position. I felt terrible. If I hurried, I could catch the three o'clock train back to Paris. But I should apologize first.

I went downstairs to explain, what, exactly, I didn't know. The madder Papa got, the harder Didi laughed.

"Ab?" Didi asked me.

"Yeah, ab. Up, right?"

"Ab?" he asked again, red faced with laughter.

"Yes, Didi, ab, ab!" I yelled, sounding like Papa.

"Ab, in German," he started, stifling more laughs, "it means down."

I looked around, but there was no hole to crawl into. Papa was still pulling glass chips out of his hair when Didi led me to the table. There were three chairs around it, and three beers on it. That's why Papa wanted the table down there, so we could all have a beer together.

Papa poured my beer slowly down the side of the glass, as if decanting a priceless Pétrus. He waited for the head to settle, then poured again, until it was perfect. We raised our glasses and clinked them.

"Prost!" Papa boomed, his voice echoing off the stone cellar walls. I froze. Didi patted me on the shoulder.

"It's okay," he said, "it means Cheers."

We drank and laughed about the whole incident. Didi and I took turns plucking glass out of Papa's scalp. And it ended well with beer from Papa's private stock. I'd move a table for Papa anytime.

After a second beer, we picked up Jörg and roared down the autobahn to Munich. Peter greeted us with open arms and beer. My kind of guy. He introduced me to his girlfriend, Amel.

They were a striking couple. Peter, all blue eyes and blond hair with a bit of the blarney in him. Amel was dark, with a radiant face and cascades of wavy black hair. They adored each other. She laughed at his endless jokes, he always wanting to hold her hand.

There's no better way to take a walking tour of Munich than with Peter. He played fast and loose with facts as we strolled through Marienplatz, Promenadeplatz, and Maximillianstraße, but nobody cared. Most of

Munich is glaringly modern, from its business district out to the infamous Olympic stadium of 1972.

Suddenly, Peter turned on me. "We used to have an old town until you Americans bombed everything!"

Amel yanked Peter aside and admonished him like a child. He bent over spewing his anger as if in pain, his eyes red and watering. The rest of us stared at the ground. Didi suggested a friendly tennis match, then dinner. I skipped tennis. I can't play anyway, and would be further hobbled by wearing blue jeans, a ratty sweatshirt, and clodhopper travel shoes.

THE BROTHERS OF SAN REMO

San Remo is an Italian restaurant run by two brothers with an unusual system. One cooks and serves wine, the other takes orders and serves food. When customers want to pay up, the chef shifts to the register, and his brother vanishes into thin air.

Several tables were pushed together when I arrived, and most of Didi's friends were already eating and into the various uncorked Barolos and Chiantis.

I poured some wine and ordered a bottle of water. Ten minutes later, nothing. I repeatedly failed to catch the waiter's eye, while Didi entertained everyone with the "Ab, ab!" story.

Everyone had their favorite; Ana with the bucket, Framboise with Crêpe Grarn Marn yarn yer ray, Sandra with the deux/douze heures mix-up at Versailles, and now Didi with "Ab, ab, *scheiße!*"

When the chef manned the register, I stepped in front of the paying customers and asked for water. He pointed to his brother and returned to the kitchen without a word.

I returned to our table and flopped down in my chair. Everyone was laughing, but I didn't know why. The waiter cleared their plates and handed out dessert menus as if I wasn't there. Amel had had enough. Not that she felt bad, her sides ached from laughing. She whispered in the waiter's ear, then signaled to the chef. A few minutes later I had water, wine, and pasta.

I got the lowdown. Thirty years ago when the brothers emigrated to Munich from Italy, they fulfilled their lifelong dream of owning a restaurant together. One evening a beautiful woman entered and dined alone. Both were smitten and each secretly dreamed of walking down the aisle with her. She turned out to be quite the two-timer, and when the brothers figured it out, they stopped talking to each other. Not a word between them in thirty years.

In order to save the restaurant, they came up with a unique solution. One brother cooks and mans the register. The other waits tables and delivers wine. If you order from the wrong brother, you can wait until Kingdom come and it will never arrive because they have no intention of delivering the message to his two-timing SOB brother. And vice-versa. Not an ideal situation in which to run a restaurant, but the food is worth it, so you put up with it.

****

We headed back to Ulm on the autobahn. We recounted the day, but were miffed at Peter's outburst. Something didn't seem right about him. Didi would call Amel and see if she could shed any light.

Rather than going home, we pulled up in front of a bar. Ulm is a small town, at least by American standards, maybe a hundred thousand residents, including the outlying areas. It has a small town feel, particularly when you enter a bar with Didi. Everyone knows him.

We pushed some tables together and before I could sit, there were beer, spritzers, and coffees all around. I didn't speak German, but Germans have an affinity for English, and luckily most at the table spoke it well.

Everyone was interested how Didi and I knew each other, and were impressed that we had met in language school in Paris. As they grasped that I lived there, chairs scooted in closer to find out where exactly, and when it might be available for some long-weekend visitors.

The next few days were a blur of walking in the old town, then ducking into a café for an espresso and pastry. Didi, like most Germans, can't go more than an hour without espresso, and I'm not far behind.

I could have stayed longer. Didi offered me his second bedroom for as long as I wanted, but I missed my apartment. As strong as the urge was to get out of Paris, I needed more strongly to return. I had done exactly what that teacher advised, and she was right.

But Didi had one last thing for us to do before I hopped on the train home. A German breakfast. Even driving in the car, the idea of a special breakfast had a different feel. First off, we returned to one of the cafés we'd spent quite a bit of time in. We bellied up to the bar and Didi ordered two breakfast specials. We talked for a bit, then I saw heaven coming toward me.

The bartender delivered two plates, each with two German white sausages, a crusty bread roll, and a beer. It was eight in the morning and I couldn't think of anything better to eat for breakfast. I could sleep on the train.

I got a lesson on proper application of mustard on the roll, and placement of the *wurst*. But I needed no instruction on the beer. It was cold, crisp, and delicious. I could have sat there all day and talked with Didi, but it was time to say good-bye and get on my way.

There was a parking spot right in front of the Hauptbahnhof. We walked in and realized it was time to say good-bye. Like Mark, we had become fast friends, and we were already planning the next time to get together, in Ulm or Paris, it made no difference. Didi chose Paris. Everybody chooses Paris.

F̶R̶I̶E̶N̶D̶!

On the train ride back I wanted to sleep. Must have been that second beer at breakfast. As my head dipped, a small hand twisted my nose and pulled, followed by giggles. There were twin five-year-old girls sitting behind me. They got right to the point.

"Maman et papa sont divorcés!" they screamed in unison. Mom and dad were divorced. They were going to visit Daddy in a petite village near Paris. I got a rundown of Daddy's new squeeze, right down to her recently purchased bosom. Before Mommy could stop them, I learned what she wears to bed when Uncle Pierre, with the Alfa Romeo, visits late at night.

Before long, they were on either side of me. We played games, laughed at my awful drawing ability, and spoke of things five-year olds find interesting, which is everything. I was never so relaxed speaking French. I made mistakes, but they didn't care. They just wanted to talk. Girls.

As badly as I wanted to get back to my apartment, I really wanted to see this thing play out. Sure enough, Daddy was waiting on the platform with his buxom babe. No doubt it was going to be an interesting weekend.

Mom collected her girls and thanked me. She'd needed some calm before the storm. One twin quickly kissed me on the cheek, and, not to be outdone, the other one followed. I waved to them through the window, and they waved back until the train pulled out.

With an hour to go until Paris, I was exhausted. Traveling, no matter how fun, is tiring. Toss in two beers for breakfast and a set of jabbering twins, I'd need a nap before the chaos in Gare de l'Est. I snuggled into my seat and pulled down the window shade. As my eyelids started their downward journey, I saw someone approaching down the aisle. He was heading right for me, and it didn't look good.

He seemed to have all his life's possessions stuffed in an oversized backpack. A canteen, tin cup, and a ladle hung on the outside, clanging against each other, and passengers' heads as he stumbled down the aisle.

He was what I called a "scruffer." He looked like he was on his third non-stop trip around the world. His hair hadn't been combed this century. His clothes looked like they were salvaged from a trash compacter. He might have had all his possessions with him, but they didn't include a razor, toothbrush, and as he got closer, soap or deodorant. And he was heading right for me. *Not again, I just got the dog smell off me. Don't move, keep your eyes shut.*

I squeezed them shut so hard they hurt. I opened one a slit and watched him ignore the fifty empty seats between us. He had that wide-eyed look of wanderlust, and a dull smile, from all that perspiration. He flopped down next to me with a great, smelly sigh.

His backpack was so big it pitched his head forward so that he was looking at his feet. But he seemed happy. Or high.

Don't move, maybe he'll think you're sleeping, better yet, dead.

He didn't seem to care he was staring at his worn out shoes. Perhaps he was just glad to be on the train to Paris, which is fine. But he stunk. I could put up with the smell, as long as he didn't talk to me.

"Friend!" he exclaimed.

Scheiße!

I rolled an eye toward him. His eyes were bloodshot, probably from his own fumes, and his face had an oily sheen. He was the valedictorian of the Markus School of Personal Hygiene. Who am I to say, but shouldn't you have at least a working knowledge of a language before unleashing it on strangers? I babble in French, sure, but only with friends.

"Friend?" Now it was a question. I couldn't keep my eyes shut for an hour, so I pretended to be interested in what he had to say, which wasn't much. He knew four, maybe five words in English, and interchanged them to form non-sensical questions that I had to untangle while he waited for an answer. All this with a two-beer breakfast hangover.

When I want to, I can flash the blankest face on the planet. It didn't work with him, in fact, he seemed inspired by it. He scrawled a blob on a napkin and wrote a word under it with no vowels and slashes over every letter.

"Country. Mine!" He handed me his pencil and encouraged me to write something. Shy about my pre-school level drawing skills, I wrote "US." He lit up like a firefly. "States friends my many!"

I tumbled that around until I understood that he had many friends in the States. I wondered how, smelling like he did.

Then he asked, "Lot you move?" That was "Do you travel much?" I think. He plowed on for an hour. "States work?" still baffles me, possibly "Do you work in the States?" "Blue many sky?" was "Good weather?" or not. It was the most exhausting hour of my life.

In the distance, the Eiffel Tower pierced the night sky, sending a jolt of energy through the passengers. He pulled down his life's possessions in various boxes, bags, and tubes from the overhead storage. When the conductor's voice droned that we'd be arriving soon, he lit up, ecstatic to be in Paris at last.

"Paris!" he exclaimed. "At least!"

In Gare de l'Est I slipped out the other end of the car and dashed into the Métro. Riding home, I thought about the young couple in Strasbourg, Katie from Zurich, Katrina hiking the Lake district, the Spanish woman I'd helped on her way home, Carla and Clara, Didi, Papa, Jörg, Peter, Amel, Stinky the Dog, Stinky the Man.

I exited the Métro and walked down Rue Vaugirard. It was chilly and I wanted to get home, but something stopped me dead in my tracks. My favorite thing in the world; rotisserie chicken. Several were spinning on a sidewalk spit, their skin a beautiful golden brown, the juices dripping onto a pile of potatoes at the bottom.

I stepped into the shop. The woman behind the counter eyed my backpack and summed me up perfectly.

"Vous avez voyagé, et maintenant vous êtes épuisé." Yes, I'd been traveling, and now I am tired. She asked me where I'd been as she scooped the potatoes into a container. I told her, then pointed to the chicken I wanted.

She told me she'd been to Italy once, but never Germany. She asked for a recommendation. I suggested Ulm, and make sure to have a proper German breakfast before you leave. Any problem, call my friend Didi.

She wrapped up my order and asked if I had wine to go with it.

"Oui, madame," I said, "j'ai *toujours* du vin." I *always* have wine. She laughed as she rang me up. She welcomed me back to Paris, and then I hurried home.

It felt great to be home, and I got my second wind. Unpacking could wait. What couldn't wait was the chicken and potatoes. Oh, and a chilled Chablis in the fridge.

I chopped up the chicken on a plate with the potatoes, opened the wine, and took it all into the bathroom. I grabbed a chair on the way, and threw open the window. Yes, the Tower was still there, glowing beautifully across town.

I took a long, slow, sip of the Chablis, then dug into my dinner. I washed it down with another delicious sip. I couldn't believe my good fortune; meeting wonderful people, my friends in Paris, and this view out my window.

I ate and drank slowly into the night, never taking my eyes off the Tower, and thinking about my life in Paris. When the food and wine were finished, I closed the window and headed for bed.

Goats in Trees, I Swear

Late one afternoon, still in my pajamas and watching a French soap opera, Framboise called me.

"Tu vas au Maroc."

It was a statement so far out of left field all I could say was, "What?"

"Tu vas au Maroc," she repeated.

"Huh?"

"Maroc!" she yelled.

"Just a sec." I grabbed my dictionary. I was going somewhere, just didn't know where. "What was it again?"

She was getting steamed, but she always got steamed when I couldn't understand her. "M-a-r-o-c." she spelled out, jaw clenched, I could tell. I cradled the receiver between my shoulder and ear and rifled through the pages.

"M...a...r...i.." You're getting married?

"Maroc!" I kept searching for something I recognized.

"M-a-r-i-n?" We're going to the beach at low tide?

"Non!" And then I found it, and was sorry I did.

"Morocco?"

"Oui!" Apparently I was going to Morocco with les Femmes Folles, the crazy women, as I affectionately called them. They had decided I was going with them and that was that.

I didn't know much about Morocco. I had hummed Jackson Browne's old tune about it for years, but that was as far as it went. They had made reservations for four. I should hurry down to the *agence de voyages* and pay for mine, since we were leaving in two days.

The travel agent didn't like me. With three women's names on the itinerary she was sure I was up to no good. Since buying an apple in France can take an hour, the purchase of an international flight with a partially paid record, using an American credit card, through a French travel agency, on a no-name package tour, I planned on being there for several days.

It really was just running the card through, but she had to make it difficult. Did I know these three other people, what was the reason for the trip? On and on.

I'd learned how to handle this by observing the Femmes Folles. I crossed my arms and stared at her. The French don't like that. It makes them feel silly asking their silly questions.

I knew what was next and I was prepared. She'd swipe a perfectly functioning credit card through and it would be rejected, supposedly. Did I have another? "Non," I replied, arms still folded. I did have another, but you can't give in because they'll say that one didn't work either, do you have a third?

It took two hours for this simple transaction, and I wasn't that hot on going in the first place. When I got home, I called Framboise to tell her it took two hours, but I got my ticket. She was impressed it went so quickly.

****

We all met at the airport. When we got on the plane, their three seats were all together. Mine was ten rows ahead of them. The guy next to me was frozen, staring at the back of the chair in front of him. He gripped the arm rests so tightly his knuckles were white. I said hello, but he didn't move.

A young woman on his other side kissed him. He didn't react. She told me he's terrified to fly and he won't speak until we land. "If we land," he corrected, through gritted teeth.

After customs, we were herded onto a bus. We found seats, three together in the back, me up front alone. I think the female tour guide welcomed us to Morocco. If she were speaking into a tin can, it would have been an improvement. Her voice cut out every other word.

Just before the door slammed, a man with "trouble" written all over him, hopped on and playfully squeezed her rear end. She screamed, but before she could retaliate, he burst into blistering French with a rat-a-tat tempo like a machine gun.

As he took over the festivities, his wife and two kids shoved past him and found seats at the back. He was still rat-a-tat-ting when the bus lurched forward, throwing the guide into his arms. He spun her around and started dancing with her, singing at the top of his lungs. She pushed him away and told him to sit as soon as possible. Guess where he sat? He slapped my thigh like we were old friends. He rat-a-tat-ed in my face, but all I could get was that he was from a small village in southwest France known for its unique accent.

No kidding.

The tour guide adjusted her hair and clothing, and started her introduction again. But the man's booming voice drowned her out. I hinted maybe he should shut up, but he wanted to teach me a song from his village. He hummed a few bars and slapped my thigh again, like "join in, why don'cha?"

I dug out my itinerary and read about our first stop, after climbing the Atlas Mountains, Ouarzazate. It's pronounced WAR-zah-zaht, in case you make this trip sitting next to a singing idiot and want to know how far it is.

I tapped my watch, indicating how long was the ride to Ouarzazate. The tour guide held up eight fingers, unable to yell over the off-key singing. Eight minutes didn't seem bad.

But something didn't feel right, we were maybe three minutes into our supposed eight minute journey and hadn't even left the airport. I held up eight fingers to the tour guide and mouthed "*minutes?*" She shook her head and twirled a finger around her watch.

"Hours?" I yelled.

I turned around. Framboise and Hélène, witnessing everything, were busting a gut with some new friends across the aisle. Momma was at least trying for some decorum, head down, but shoulders shaking. I gestured, anyone want to swap places? They doubled over.

I studied this guy as he trampled through some provincial anthem. I noticed, from his bristly crew-cut, to his topped-off ears, to his jaw line, everything was square. His nose was square, when he spoke his mouth was square like a robot's, his teeth were big square blocks. His arms hung from square shoulders. His kneecaps looked like he had books under his slacks. He wore square-toed shoes.

In between bouts of patriotic singing, I learned he was twice divorced, no surprise there, and seemed determined to make it a trifecta. He asked me something in his rat-a-tat voice and looked at me expectantly.

A woman behind me whispered in my ear, "He wants you to sing a song from your country."

"Not a chance," I told her, still staring at his big square smile.

We wound through the Atlas Mountains, a beautiful, desolate expanse. I hoped the girls were taking photos because it would be the only way I would see them because Square Head blocked my view.

When I could get him out of my face, I could see bits of the Draa Valley. I couldn't hear the guide over his rat-a-tat-tat, but it looked much like the American Southwest, dotted with dense clusters of date palms signaling an occasional oasis.

Several times I could see a kasbah, a stone fortress jutting out of a steep slope. Built for protection years ago, most of them still operated in some form or another. Couldn't get that part of the info because of you-know-who next to me.

My first observation of Morocco was it would be impossible for even the most vigilante equal rights advocate to make inroads in the Draa Valley. Clustered under the shade of argan trees, Berber men smoked, sipped tea, and joked around, while the women gathered and humped kindling wood, babies, and food across the desolate landscape in crippling heat.

I asked the guide, "When do the men return home?"

"When the fire is lit and the food is cooked and on the table."

"And after?"

"They go outside in the cool of the evening to smoke, sip tea, and joke around, while the women clean up and put the children to bed." And I thought I had it bad sitting next to Granite Gums.

We stopped in the middle of nowhere to appreciate the Draa's vastness. I walked to a cluster of Berber men beneath an argan tree. They were smoking some terrific smelling tobacco. Despite the heat, it was cool and pleasant in the shade. They had, as my dad used to say, the world by the ass.

I watched the women in the distance, bent over, children hanging on them, lugging wood on their backs. I figured it was as good a time as any to start something.

I opened my mouth to speak. But something hit me on the side of my head, and it hurt. I looked up. The tree was full of goats, standing on narrow branches munching on argan fruit.

These weren't cute farm goats with wispy goatees. They were the mangiest, buck-toothed goats on record. If you jammed fake hillbilly teeth in their mouths, and gave them Groucho glasses, it would be an improvement. Berber men love their goats, but they wouldn't win a beauty pageant.

One of the goats, I think it was the one with the lazy eye, had spat an argan pit at me. Lazy eye or not, he was a helluva shot. He hit me again, on the top of my head. The men got a kick out of that, slapping their thighs, passing a bottle. And why not, smoking and drinking in the shade with a buck-toothed brigade overhead protecting them?

There must have been a dozen of these goats depositing the pits in piles on the ground. When they'd finished eating the fruit on one branch, they'd gracefully walked to a new one and continue their meal.

I walked under the tree marveling at these goats, as the men stifled their laughs. It's not every day you can see goats in trees, so I ignored them. It took a minute, but I got it.

I was standing under a bunch of goats that have the manners of, let's face it, goats. After eating all that fruit, there would eventually be an intestinal blitzkrieg. And that's what the men were waiting for. It's the feeling you get when you walk into a dark alley in a strange neighborhood.

I gotta get out of here.

Plus, if these goats were as good a shot out the back, as Goofy Eye was out the front, I could be in real trouble. I backed out slowly and waved the girls over, but they didn't want to be near them. The men, not the goats. But when I got hit a third time in the back of the head, their curiosity got to them, along with the rest of our group. They circled the tree in amazement.

The tour guide explained that unlike these Berber men, the goats served a vital purpose. The pits were gathered and sold to make argan oil for cosmetics and cooking. No surprise, the women collected the pits and took them to market.

I was about to ask a question when I got hit again. Goofy Eye stared me down, one eye on me, the other on a passing jetliner at 35,000 feet. I don't know how he did it. It was like shooting a rifle with a bent scope. Don't believe me? Search "goats in trees."

****

I've never had a problem with a city's meaning or catchphrase. City of Light, the Big Apple, I get it. I've always felt that Philadelphia was yanking the nation's chain with City of Brotherly Love. But Ouarzazate means, Without Confusion.

When our bus entered the city limits, children ran alongside pounding its sides, jumping in front to force us to stop, hands out. We stopped at a souk, an outdoor market. Rat-a-tat couldn't wait to get off and join the throngs.

He banged on the door for the driver to let him out, then stepped into a shouting storm of humanity, and couldn't have been happier. He bought all sorts of junk, rat-a-tatting away, pointing, singing that damn song, and then danced with a group of kids over to another vendor.

We watched him from the safety of our bus, asking questions, negotiating prices, and piling up merchandise, not knowing a word of Arabic.

He jangled and rattled back onto the bus wearing some sort of watchman's cap with netting all around. He tried to put it on me.

"Get away!"

"Rat-a-tat?" he asked.

"No!" He turned to a lady on the other side.

"Rat-a-tat?"

"Non!"

He put it back on, but no matter how he arranged it, the round hat wouldn't fit on his square head.

We had an hour to unpack at the hotel until it was time for dinner. I suggested the girls go without me, I'd eat something out of the honor bar. Momma pointed out there wasn't one, so we dined, sitting on the floor, like kings and queens, on couscous, vegetables, and delicious flatbread. My only complaint was they forgot chairs and silverware.

The next day we visited a kasbah, a spice market, and a royal palace, then dined on the floor around a table overflowing with Moroccan specialties; lamb, tajine, and salads infused with ginger and paprika. But again, no silverware.

After dinner, the local armory put on a wonderful show of horsemanship and ceremony, firing rifles into the night sky while maneuvering deftly in procession. After they dismounted to answer questions, Square Mouth asked if he could shoot a rifle. They dismissed him like a petulant child and ordered him to go away. I have great respect for the Moroccan armory.

The next morning we headed out to Taroudant past kasbahs, oases, and more tea-drinking Berber and goats. We detoured onto a rutted road, kicking up dust and gravel.

Square Ears thought it was great fun bouncing about, singing, wearing that stupid hat. We stepped out into a dust cloud, choking and waving to clear the air. When it cleared, there was a sea of merchants hawking their cheap wares.

Women knelt on blankets in the gravel, waving us over for a look. Two men grappled with an anxious camel, his tongue slumped out the side of his mouth like a dead salmon. His teeth looked like he flossed with a chain saw. He must have had the same dentist as the goats.

The girls and I backed away from the camel until we stepped onto something soft. Hélène turned and gasped. Ouarzazate is called the Door of the Desert, and for good reason.

The gravel gave way to an ocean of sand. Rippling dunes rolled to the horizon in endlessly shifting waves. We stood there, numb from the beauty. To our left and right the sand formed a smooth, endless shore line. We were straddling the edge of civilization, and the beginning of the great Sahara Desert.

I dipped my toe in. It was warm and soft, and I felt like I was the first person in the world to step there. At that moment it was silent, no screaming children, no women hawking their wares. I looked up.

Something was bouncing along the horizon, and something billowing behind it. It reversed, and headed toward us, kicking up a sand storm. Four gangly legs galloped independently, like an old mare running from the glue factory.

It was the camel. It had broken loose from its handlers, but not before Framboise somehow got on his back wearing a purple turban that was unraveling behind her.

We didn't realize how fast the beast was moving until it roared past us and crashed into the marketplace. Dust and rocks and trinkets exploded into the air. The two handlers huffed past us, swiping at the ropes and trailing turban.

Not causing enough calamity on the first pass, the camel stumbled through again crushing everything in sight, and spitting at us like a paintball shooter.

The Paris-Dakar road rally couldn't have kicked up more debris. Women grabbed their children and ran. The bus driver hopped in his bus and shut the door.

In a tornado of dust, the camel lumbered back into the Sahara, his tongue flopping like a fish on a line. Framboise held on, screaming like a banshee.

As I watched her disappear into the Sahara, I realized it was nice knowing her. She had befriended me on the street, brought me into her circle of friends, and had made my time in Paris a life-changing experience. But now she was disappearing into the Sahara on a crazed camel.

The camel couldn't keep up the frantic pace, but they'd make the Algerian border by dawn. They speak French there, so maybe she could help a tourist order a crêpe on the street.

And then the damned thing turned around and headed for us again. We all ran to the bus and pounded on the door. Some got in, but most of us hid behind it in horror, as the gangly thing thundered through again. But this time it skidded to a stop and dropped its front legs and head, exhausted.

Framboise pitched forward and slid down its neck into the arms of the handlers, grinning from ear to ear. Square Head was on her like white on rice.

"Rat-a-tat-tat-tat-a-tat?" he asked.

Framboise shoved him away and made her way toward us, uncoiling the rest of the turban. It had to be fifty feet long. One of the handlers rolled it into a ball behind her. When he gathered the last of it, he tapped her on the shoulder. He wanted to be paid.

Apparently, while the rest of us were marveling at the ocean of sand before us, Framboise was deep into negotiations for a camel ride. Before the fee could be paid, the dumb thing took off.

Hélène, Momma, and I pooled our money and came to an agreeable sum. We refused to let Framboise pay. My stomach rolled over as I thought of Yoko, and now Framboise, and I realized how glad I was she was safe.

After that we visited another kasbah, an ancient pool of fertility, and sacred rooms walled in mosaics. We sat by a wellspring for an impromptu lunch. We toured the Oasis de Fint, where you step into another world of lush vegetation and life, away from the unforgiving desert. We crossed the Sous Valley, and on entering Taroudant we sensed excitement in the air.

Banners in Arabic were strung across the main street. We learned a parade was set up for a foreign dignitary. Police were out in force, but the crowds were well-behaved as long as you didn't try to push to the front. Which we did. How often do you get to see a visiting dignitary?

Music poured out of loudspeakers lining the route. The police took hardened stances. I got my camera ready as I saw the motorcade turn onto the main street. People began waving and jumping and cheering.

I got jostled a bit, but restrained from pushing back. Not here. Not now. I squinted into my viewfinder and zoomed in as tightly as I could on the lead car. A convertible, with flags all around, and bunting pouring over the side.

I saw a man with bushy dark hair, dressed in flowing white, sitting on the trunk with his legs dangling into the back seat. He was waving at the crowd left and right. Big smile. As he got closer the crowed roared their approval.

A chill ran up my back. I couldn't believe what I saw in my viewfinder. I dropped the camera and stared dumbfounded as the car rolled past not ten feet from me. It was Moammar Gadhafi. He looked right at me and waved.

And then he was gone. Suddenly I didn't want to be trapped with these frenzied people. I backed away from the curb. The girls were already a safe distance away. They had seen him too. The only thing I regret is I didn't take that photo. No one would believe me otherwise. But ask the girls, they'll tell you.

After a Libyan lunatic smiles at you in a parade, there isn't much else to do. We rode the bus to Agadir, a beach resort on the North Atlantic. It was a day to gather ourselves and think about what an interesting trip it turned out to be.

We couldn't sit by the pool. Square Trunks was on the high dive, teaching the hired help how to cannonball, splashing down like a sack of potatoes. So we packed our bags and enjoyed our last lunch together and hurried to pack for our flight home that evening.

On the plane, I sat next to the poor young man with the fear of flying. His girlfriend stroked his hair, trying to soothe him, but nothing helped. We walked out of the airport with them and wished them well.

On the way home I bought some cold cuts and a baguette and hurried home. I dragged a chair into the bathroom and opened the window. The night was clear and cool. The Eiffel Tower was still there, beautiful as ever. What a view. "A view with a room," I chuckled, as I popped the wine cork.

I tore off a chunk of bread and tucked some sliced meat into it. I washed it down with a nice red Rhône. I leaned back. "I'll be damned," I said out loud, "Moammar goddamn Gadhafi."

A Night at the Opera

A friend, whom I could strangle, recommended I go see the play *Orpheus aux Enfers*, Orpheus in the Underworld, at the Palais Garnier, the Paris Opera House. It had gotten good reviews for its unusual take on the venerable story, so what better way to spend Christmas Eve than in the legendary home of the world's most famous Phantom? When I had stopped by the box office I was surprised to find a seat available at such short notice.

I was in fine form when I stepped off the Métro wearing my best, and headed into the lobby flashing my ticket. It was exciting rubbing elbows with assorted snobs and "pseuds" as John Lennon called them.

I maneuvered around the ruffled clothing and stale perfume, but soon left that dog and pony show, and headed for my box.

I entered a small dark room with ten plush, red seats. The walls were covered in red velvet. I half expected a Madame to enter with scantily-clad young women from whom I could choose.

I scooted down the aisle and sat. Right behind an enormous supporting column. No wonder the ticket was available, and cheap. I was so close to the column I had to straddle it and lean around it to see. Hard on the back.

On my left was a woman holding opera glasses in one hand, and a cigarette in a foot-long holder in the other. To my right was a man wearing a toupée that looked like he'd won it in a raffle. Or a tug-of-war. The lights went down, the curtain went up, and I couldn't see.

I'll be brief, because the play wasn't. The Statue of Liberty ascended from the bowels of the stage in a puff of smoke. A dwarf entered wearing an eagle's head. He argued with a silver-painted mailman with winged feet tossing glitter on the audience. A naked lady argued with them, then ran off with a moose wearing Bermuda shorts. End of Act I. One hour down, and according to the program, two to go.

During the break, the lady next to me asked if I thought the naked woman should stay with the moose long term. I told her I didn't care who she ended up with, as long as she came back out a few more times. She turned away in disgust. I turned to the toupée. "I'm confused," I whispered, "is Orpheus the mailman or the moose?"

"Pardon?"

"And another thing," I went on in my halting French, "is the stage the underworld, or are we in the underworld? Because if we are, I get it. My back's killing me."

He cocked his head like an inquisitive dog. For ten minutes we searched for common ground, but never found it. But when the smoking woman piped in with her disgust at my inability to understand the subtext of a moose in Bermuda shorts making time with a naked lady, it was time to leave. Besides, it was Christmas Eve.

I walked out into the chilly Paris evening and took an outside table at a small café on Rue de la Paix. I had a terrific meal of wine, a plate of charcuterie, a little more wine, some chèvre chaud, a little more wine, dessert, then a little more wine.

I walked down the busy streets towards the Seine. People were out in droves, beautifully dressed, and in good cheer. I strolled down the quays. Traffic was horrible, and it was a bear crossing Pont Saint-Michel, but no better time to visit Nôtre Dame.

There was a long line outside the cathedral, and it was jammed when I got inside, but I had nothing else to do. A million candles flickered shadows on the dark walls. I shuffled along with the crowd as a choir sang. But by the time we circled behind the main altar, I'd had enough. It seemed all of Paris was inside.

I crossed the Seine to the Latin Quarter and entered tiny Saint-Julien-le-Pauvre. It's much smaller than Nôtre Dame, but just as beautiful. Here was a neighborhood church. The priest spoke slowly and I understood nearly everything, even with the echo.

But I can only take so much of being told what a disappointment we are to our Maker, even on the eve of His birth, so I headed back out into the cold. Snowflakes swirled around me, dusting everything in white.

In the Latin Quarter, a children's choir sang sweetly. They kept their eyes glued to their teacher, looking down occasionally at the words in their hymnals. You could tell who the parents were, eyes riveted on their child with smiles brighter than any candle. An elderly woman accidentally bumped into me. She didn't say "excusez-moi," but rather "joyeux noël" and moved on.

I had never spent a Christmas wandering aimlessly, let alone in Paris. It was cold, and crowded, and noisy, and I highly recommend it. The Saint-Michel Métro was closed. A taxi would be impossible on such a night, so I strolled down Saint-Germain.

I looked in dark store windows, read posters taped to nightclub walls, and watched cars pass by. I angled over to the general direction of home, and kept walking. This time I paid attention to where I was going. I didn't think I'd meet another set of cops like before.

When I got home, my legs ached and I was cold, but when I warmed up, I was famished. There was an inch of wine in a bottle, some bread and cheese. It was becoming a habit, but I gathered it all up and dragged a chair into my bathroom.

I opened the window and sat. The Tower was dusted white but still glowed amber underneath. The city left it on all night for this special time of year, or possibly just for me. Possibly. I don't know what it is about that hunk of metal, but I couldn't get enough of it.

I could still hear those children's voices singing in my head. I folded the bread around the cheese and dipped it in the wine.

I thought about the night of my party when we all took turns at the window, Ana on Juan's shoulders directing traffic, Didi interpreting for Ignacio. I wondered what they were doing right now. I missed them. I finished the wine and headed for bed. A perfect Christmas.

When Bobby Came to Visit

Whether it's fun having friends visit you in Paris depends on who your friends are. With spring just around the corner, Bobby called one morning. We had worked together in what seemed like a former life. He was in London on business. I have no idea how he got my number, but that's Bobby. If you live in Paris, your phone number will spread like wildfire, whether you like it or not.

Bobby had the weekend off and wanted to visit. Bobby was fun in the way it's fun when your hamster gets loose. Problem was, Markus had booked himself a corner of my living room weeks earlier. I wasn't sure how the two would mix, Bobby high-strung and groomed to perfection, Markus, half his age and with a bathing-optional lifestyle.

If I made a list who I thought would ask to spend a weekend in Paris, Markus would be dead last. He never seemed interested in Paris or learning French. He was eighteen years old, and spent all his free time scouring obscure movie houses for his all-time favorite film, *Critters*. It stood alone in his private pantheon of cinema. No other movie came close, except when *Critters 2* debuted.

Bobby arrived first. We were getting caught up on our lives when there was a knock at my door. Well, I thought, here goes nothing. After I introduced them, they ignored me, yammering away like childhood friends, Bobby loud and direct, Markus replying in his raspy "Yes-yes!" I never saw two people bond faster. I had to pry them off the couch to go to dinner. Bobby grabbed his fifty-foot muffler and wrapped it around and around and around, as I pushed them out the door.

At dinner I was fascinated watching them. Neither spoke a word of the other's language, so they jabbered in a cryptic code while air drawing their thoughts. They'd quickly dispensed with the courtesies of polite conversation and were into the meat and potatoes: female anatomy.

In the middle of the meal, Bobby stood up and pointed to his butt and asked Markus, "What's this in German?" Markus told him. Bobby repeated it five times so it would sink in, then it was Markus's turn. Back and forth it went all through the meal. In one of my favorite restaurants, where I can probably never return.

Occasionally there would be a blip and they'd stare blankly at each other. Bobby would scrawl a body part on a napkin, and Markus would blurt "Yes-yes!" and they'd move on. The waiter wanted to throw them out but held his tongue, knowing me from previous uneventful dinners.

After anatomy class, I asked what they wanted to do later. They had already discussed it, and I had no say in the matter.

"Hookers! Yes-yes!" Markus said, almost jumping out of his seat. And now it made sense why Markus had returned to Paris. He was here for his first time. Well, if you're going to do it, I guess it should be in Paris. And then he headed for the bathroom.

Bobby paid the bill to mitigate the damages that were sure to follow. Starting with Markus taking too long in the bathroom. The men waiting in line were getting restless.

Bobby went to check on him, which with Bobby, is never a good idea. He shoved to the front of the line and pounded on the bathroom door. I sprinted over just as the door flew open. And that's when the fight started.

They barked at each other in their own languages like junkyard dogs. When the French men and tourists joined in, with their bladders bursting, it sounded like a U.N. dispute. I pulled Bobby back to our table.

"Do you know what that nut was doing in there?" he asked me. I was pretty sure I did. Markus had initiated Round One in the bathroom in order to extend his pleasure with some lucky gal later on. Bobby had interrupted Markus, and he wasn't happy. Oh, to be eighteen again.

Markus flopped into his chair, cheeks flushed, and dug into his dessert with a child's innocence. Bobby was about to light into him, but he mulled the kid's logic and beamed like a proud father.

"That takes guts, you son of a bitch." Bobby mussed Markus's hair.

"Yes-yes!" Markus said, scraping the last bits of dessert from his bowl. Bobby wiped his hand on his napkin.

"But one of these days you gotta take a bath."

It was a beautiful evening so we decided to walk. Bobby and Markus walked ten steps ahead of me jabbering like school girls. I couldn't lose them, with Bobby's muffler trailing behind. Occasionally he'd stumble over it. I'd catch up as he'd untangle it from his leg, or someone else's. Bobby, the Fashionista.

I stopped halfway across the Alexander III bridge over the Seine. My heart soared. Paris is always beautiful, but that night was exceptional. It looked like a painting.

Art nouveau lamps bathed the bridge in a frosty glow. On the quays, lovers held hands and stole kisses. Upriver, Bateaux Mouches plied the water, pushing shimmering waves to the shore. It was stunning. But not as stunning as when I turned around.

Bobby had mounted one of the bridge's cherub statues from behind and was giving Markus pointers on proper hip thrust while he spanked the angel's rump. In the other hand, he twirled a phantom lasso overhead.

"Bobby!" I screamed, horrified. "Get down!"

"Just a sec," Bobby calmly said. He scooted around to the cherub's front to continue his impromptu sex class. Uh oh, I thought, the hamster was loose. As usual with Bobby, a crowd gathered. Some laughed, some snapped photos. One nut shot some video. And why not, who would believe it back home?

By the time I fought through the crowd, Bobby was leaning against the statue with a post-coitus cigarette and had everyone in stitches, saying how his little angel was coy, and a bit frumpy for his taste, but all in all not bad.

So much for Paris at dusk.

We didn't need signs pointing to Saint-Denis, the red-light district; we just followed the freaks. At first it wasn't bad, but as we got deeper into it, the outfits got more daring and gender lines blurred.

By the time we stopped on a corner in the thick of it, it was a Fellini film, only weirder. Bobby sized up every one, and every thing, that passed. How in the world did I end up here? I wondered. Oh, that's right, Bobby's in town.

Bobby threw a fatherly arm around Markus. "Choose carefully kid, your first time only comes around once."

Bobby, the Philosopher.

Markus found who, or what, he wanted, in a chaotic mix of Caribbean islands wearing a sequined dress built to be shed quickly. I watched my former classmate hold his own with the negotiations, with Bobby sticking his nose in, nodding, making sure what was included in the base price.

Bobby, the Advisor.

Markus couldn't remember to bring a pen to class, but ordering à la carte on the mean streets of Paris he was a fierce negotiator. And just like that the deal was done.

Markus hung his coat on my arm, slipped his shoulder bag around my neck, and emptied his pockets, except for the agreed-upon cash. He followed her across the street and into a dark building like a lost puppy.

Bobby leaned on a lamppost, foot up, puffing away liked he'd lived in Paris all his life. Markus waved from a third floor window.

"Remember what I told ya', kid!" Bobby boomed, twirling that damned lasso.

"Yes-yes!"

Bobby, the Proud Father.

Then the lady lowered the shade. I hoped she had a saddle, because from the demonstration with the statue on the bridge it was going to be a bumpy ride.

Standing in a red-light district, holding someone else's belongings, I'd never been so uncomfortable. Not Bobby. He lit up again, now paying more attention to the passing merchandise.

Oh, please no.

After a few more cigarettes, Bobby got worried. "Maybe he got bashed in the head and he's dead."

Bobby, the Optimist. "Let's go find him."

"I'm not going up there. What's the matter with you?" I argued.

"Maybe you're right. Here." Bobby hung his coat on my other arm and twirled his muffler around me until I looked like I was ready for a snowstorm. He pulled out a wad of cash and stuffed his wallet in my pocket.

"Why should the kid have all the fun?" Bobby asked to no one but himself, and off he went. He disappeared around the corner with a woman in an orange 70s wig, flashing LEDs in her stockings, and live goldfish swimming in her twelve-inch Elton John platforms. And men wonder why women can't stand us.

I stood there, arms out, like a thrift store coat rack. I got heckled by two punks and propositioned by another. A homeless man pulled Bobby's coat off my arm and slipped it on. He studied himself in a store window, and spun around. He even asked me how it looked on him. In the end he decided he didn't like it, hung it back on me, and shuffled off.

I felt something on my back. I turned around. It was a pair of eyes a block away, staring at me. Worse, it was a cop, and I could tell even at this distance, we had the same thought of each other. Trouble.

As he approached, I could see he wasn't just any cop, but one who had failed to rise through the ranks like he had planned. He was too old for this beat, and the frustration over his stifled career radiated off him like heat lightning.

He approached slowly, sizing me up with each purposeful step. I scoured my brain for French words I would soon need; public defender, bail, embassy. He circled me, taking in the dangling muffler and coats, adding up the endless violations that would follow. After his third spin, he had no more idea what to do with me than before. Technically, I wasn't breaking any laws. Yet.

What bothered me was that all the pink boas, fishnets, and teddies drumming up business got a free pass, but a human clothes rack, doing nothing wrong, and wanting nothing more than to get out of there, got the treatment.

He gestured for me to move on, as if I were a threat to the working girls wearing thongs for outerwear. I explained my situation, but he was in too deep to back off. He inspected Markus's bag, unwound Bobby's muffler, went through all my pockets, and found nothing incriminating.

"Get your hands off my coat or I'll rip your head off!" Bobby yelled as he rounded the corner, ready for a fight. With a cop. I pleaded with him not to make a fuss. He didn't have to. Markus came bopping across the street grinning from ear to ear. He'd had his day, and Bobby wanted details.

The cop was fascinated watching them trade details in their jabber-babble. I thought we might be in the clear, but they hit one of their blips. Bobby looked around, I suppose for another cherub statue to mount, and settled for a fire hydrant. He climbed on and recounted his adventure with Miss Goldfish Shoes, spanking her, then sliding around to the front. The cop looked at me, speechless.

Markus pulled Bobby off the hydrant and hopped on. As he began his demo, I thought of the poor woman who took him up to that third floor window. He swung his leg over. I wasn't sure how he started, but now he seemed to be facing backward. Bobby was so impressed with his protégé, he turned to the cop.

"Hey, what do you call that in French?" Bobby asked, pointing to Markus violating the hydrant like a squirrel in heat. The cop mumbled something. Whatever Markus was doing, backward or forward, had a word in French, and Bobby wanted to know it.

Bobby pulled a pen out of his coat and handed it to the cop. "Write it on my hand, would 'ya? I want to remember it." The cop, baffled by the whole thing, scribbled on Bobby's hand. Bobby took a stab at pronouncing it, but couldn't. He held his hand up to my face, wanting me to pronounce it.

"Not now," I pleaded, "Let's get out of here."

And just like that it was over. The two Casanovas retrieved their belongings from their personal valet, and headed out of Saint-Denis, ten steps in front of me. They playfully bumped each other, then stopped for one of their linguistic blips, and continued on, laughing, bonded by a night of debauchery. When I turned around at the next block, the cop was still looking at us.

We found a bar and toasted Markus. I thought we'd stay a while and have a few too many, but it was his night. We spent the next four hours in a noisy Pigalle video arcade. No Champagne. No talk. Just Kung Fu Killers and a pocket of coins.

On Top of Samaritaine

Everyone has their favorite viewing point to look out over Paris. The Eiffel Tower, of course, comes to mind, but you have to ride in a terrifyingly small box-elevator, straight up. And when you get there, it's packed with people, and it's either windy, or cold, or both. And in the back of your mind is the hellish ride down that awaits.

The Arc has a good view of the Champs Elysées and La Défense, but not much else. The Pantheon feels far removed. Montmartre could be terrific, but the trees and apartments block most of the view. The best thing about the view from the top of the ugly black Tour Montparnasse is you don't see the ugly black Tour Montparnasse. It just feels wrong being in a building that should never have been built.

I like the view from the top of the department store Samaritaine. Maybe it's the oddity of walking past makeup and jewelry displays on the way up. Whatever it is, once you step onto the roof, you feel right in the middle of everything.

There's a makeshift café on top. I come up here a lot. I watch the barista's irritance at people staying too long, hogging the view. But me he leaves alone. Most shoppers inside don't know, or don't care, what's up here. But I care. And if you follow the small signs and make all the right turns, you can order a drink and watch Paris go by on a rooftop.

It's a place where you can think. Lately I'd been thinking my days were numbered and passing too quickly. I avoided thinking of when my money would run out and I would have to leave. The money was thin and I wasn't having much success teaching English to children whose parents had posted 3x5 cards at the American Church. The problem was the parents wanted their children to learn English. The children didn't.

Everyone has their own definition of wasting time. More than a few would think sitting on a department store rooftop was the definitive waste of time. Not me. I could look at Paris all day and return home satisfied.

As often as I had visitors stay with me, I never brought them up here. What's sounds more fun, a walk through the catacombs, or Samaritaine? A midnight bowl of onion soup and Champagne at Beaubourg, or Samaritaine?

My only problem was, how many more times could I come up here? Would I remember this view years from now? And why didn't I come up here more often? But I do come up often, just not enough.

On this particular day I had gone to my bank. I was shocked to see how low my account was. I watched it like a hawk, but it was going faster than I planned. Setting aside the rent and food ration budget, I thought I should've had twice what was in there. But I didn't.

In the beginning, a year seemed like a long time. But summer flew by with school and parties, and fall was filled with travel, snails, and Dominique, sort of. Winter was Mont St. Michel, Augustin's jokes, Christmas, and the oddest play I'd ever seen. Spring started fittingly with Markus's day in the sun, but where did the time go? And what would I do with the precious little that was left? I thought of the guy on the plane coming over.

"Then what...?"

A lot, it turned out. And that was what I was contemplating on the top of Samaritaine that day.

Jane, a Balloon, and Marvin

Sometimes things just happen. You don't know why they happen, they just do. I needed some cheering up and thought I'd visit Mark in England. He had to give his friend a ride up to Scotland. I could tag along, and we could cross over to Ireland. Apparently there was a pub or two in Dublin he hadn't been to.

I wanted to enjoy the journey, so instead of flying, I booked a bus to Calais to catch the ferry to Dover, then on to London, then Yorkshire.

It was an unusually hot spring afternoon, so of course, one hour into the four hour ride, the bus lost power, forcing the driver to shut off the air conditioning. We lumbered along at a snail's pace; hermetically sealed inside.

I looked around at the other passengers. It was so French, everyone reading or talking, perspiring like they'd just stepped out of the shower, which, from the ripe odor, few of them had.

I squirmed in my moist seat, mopping my forehead. A woman behind me lit a cigarette and blew smoke over the back of my seat. I could feel it stick to my neck.

The woman next to me seemed to be the only other person who was miserable. She kept dabbing her face with a tissue, but it was already soaked. In the best of situations I'm not a conversationalist, but I couldn't take it any longer.

"I've never been so uncomfortable in my life," I croaked, surprised at my raspy voice.

"I *kahnt* breathe a lick," she said right back. It was the *kahnt* that I knew we were heading to her native England. "The bloody French with their airs. Say what you want about us Brits, but if the air doesn't work, you can bloody well bet we wouldn't sit like nothing was wrong."

Another nicotine cloud swirled past. The woman next to me twisted out of her seat and stared down the smoking woman. "Good heavens, what on earth is wrong with you?"

The smoker's eyes bugged out. She yanked the cigarette out of the smoker's mouth, snuffed it out, and tossed it back in her lap. She flopped back into her seat next to me and dabbed her forehead. "Bloody French."

And that's how I met Jane.

"Got any water?" I squeaked. She held up her empty bottle.

"Gone before we left Paris. At this rate we won't get to London before dark."

She was right. It was a four hour ride if the bus was zooming through the French countryside, which it wasn't. The driver opened the doors up front, but it did nothing. There was no rear door to let the air flow through. So we gasped and squirmed and dabbed, hoping that over the next hill we might see the English Channel.

And we did. Seven hours later.

Exhausted, and I wasn't half way to my destination. At Calais we were herded onto the ferry. Jane and I found each other on the outside deck. We couldn't get enough fresh air. By the time we pulled into London we knew a lot about each other.

Jane was a hot air balloon pilot. She had a few days off to visit her family outside London. When we parted ways, I had her company's phone number in the Loire Valley, and a veiled threat that if I didn't come down to the Valley of Kings, dire consequences were in the offing.

And that is how I found myself, with my precious days winding down, on a train to the small village of Limeray in the Loire. When I arrived at the station I showed the taxi driver my scribbled piece of paper. He knew the address.

We took off like a rocket, or as fast as a two-cylinder tin can could, and roared through town. We scattered some chickens crossing the road and skidded to a stop on a bridge. He pointed to the sky.

"Monsieur! Les gonfliers!" Up high was a multi-colored hot air balloon drifting silently over the Loire River, its bright colors reflecting off the water like a mirror.

It was enormous, but graceful as a ballerina. You could hear glasses clinking as the passengers in the basket sipped Champagne and gasped at the view. My driver waved his beret like a child. "Salut, mes amis! Salut!" He ran to the front of his car and waved one last time before the balloon disappeared over the trees.

A few minutes later we skidded to a stop on a narrow street of homes. The front door flew open and there was Jane looking smart in a white shirt with gold bars, black tie, and khaki slacks. I almost saluted. She grabbed my bag and I entered a house full of airship captains and crew.

They were an interesting group. Most were English, over for the spring and summer, flying or chasing balloons over the French countryside. The house, a perk for working for the company, was decorated dormitory style, right down to cinder blocks and boards for shelves.

Pillows and rugs were scattered across the living room where everyone sat around recounting the day's adventures. And they had a chef, a Swiss beauty, who had worked her way around the world cooking for royalty. She grew tired of it and settled down in the Loire with one of the airship captains. It's the uniform. It's always the uniform.

Before I could say hello, I was swept into the backyard and offered a plate of crudités, a baguette, and a glass of Vouvray. But it would be no leisurely afternoon. There was a problem.

A balloon was scheduled to set down in forty-five minutes, but the walkie-talkies had gone dead and nobody could find it. Sheesh, I thought, as I ripped off a chunk of baguette and washed it down with the chilled wine, feet up on the table like the king of France, how hard can it be to find a hot air balloon? Look up, for cryin' out loud. But I didn't say anything. Instead I poured a second glass of Vouvray.

Jane wasn't flying that day. She drove the chase van. Before I could top off my wine glass (there was only an inch left, I swear), she handed me binoculars and ordered me into the van.

Off we went, with the crew stuffed in back. Jane sped down a bumpy road with one hand on the wheel, and barked into her walkie with the other, trying to contact the missing flight crew. No response.

My orders were to scan the skies, but I couldn't figure out how something as big as what I saw from the taxi could be so hard to find. But thirty minutes later, not a trace.

I was a bit tipsy, and the binoculars kept banging my head as I searched the skies. I couldn't find a balloon a hundred feet up, but I found the sun ninety-two million miles away. I was blinking away blue spots when Jane jerked the van onto a rocky path.

"There they are," she said.

"Oh yeah, right," I mumbled, still blinking away spots under my eyelids.

We rounded a bend and skidded to a stop. The balloon was gently ruffling on the ground, purging its last gasps of magical air that made it soar only moments ago. Now just an acre of billowing fabric.

Ballooning is not an exact science. You set a plan where you want to go, but really you're beholden to the winds and pulling a few ropes. Sometimes the balloon just goes where it pleases. It's no big deal, except when the walkies go dead, and the captain can't tell you where he landed, and the chase scout (me) can find the sun, but nothing closer.

The passengers were sitting in the tall grass flush with excitement. They didn't know the walkies were dead and that they were actually lost for a while, and Jane wanted to keep it that way.

"Grab the bubbly, would you, love?" Jane ordered me. Normally the chase van arrives before the landing, and has Champagne on ice waiting. "Sorry folks, my fault. Should've had more petrol in the tank!" Jane lied, covering up. But no one minded after seeing chilled Moët dangling from each of my hands.

By the time the bottles were empty (they didn't offer me any), the sun was sinking fast and the night chill was coming on. I helped fold an acre of silk into a surprisingly small bundle, and stuffed it into the back of the van. The basket rode on top, the passengers in the back, flush with Champagne and an unforgettable sunset ride in the sky.

****

The sun hadn't come up yet when someone kicked my makeshift bed. "Get up, mate," someone whispered in the dark. "You're going flying." I forced a puffy eye open. Everyone was stumbling in the dark in various stages of dress.

We sat outside in the pre-dawn chill and I couldn't imagine why we were up so early. I heard a faint squeak as one of the captains plucked a tiny duckling out of a plastic pool and plopped him on the table. Someone had found Marvin by the side of the road, and had brought him home. He was their mascot who, when the boss wasn't looking, rode in the balloon. They had bets when he would leap out and soar off.

Marvin was partial to the crusty ends of baguettes, so mornings were a treat. He loved to sit in your hand, he was that small, and wait for a morsel. But it made eating awkward. So he learned to sit in the crook of your foot. If you crossed your legs you could gently swing him as he tested his wings. When he finished eating, he'd flop to the ground and crawl back into his pool, and paddle in circles. I liked Marvin.

In the van, Jane filled me in with what I would be required to know. "Grab a rope and hold on like bloody hell," was the main thing.

The young passengers had more Champagne than breakfast for their Champagne breakfast, and couldn't wait to board. But there was work to do. We unrolled the balloon fabric and checked for damage. Jane attached cables to it and lit the burners. The rest of us held up the edges to trap the hot air.

After thirty minutes, the balloon was full and wanted to take off. The basket bobbed as Jane helped the two passengers inelegantly swing their legs over the side and flop in. She made a final check and signaled me to cast off. The basket rose so slowly, they had cleared the trees before they realized they'd left the ground.

The rest of us climbed into the van and returned to the house for coffee. Once the balloon is in the air, there's nothing to do until it lands. We sat in the backyard, and

Marvin rode my foot up and down, fluttering his wings for that day he would soar. I didn't share his joy. I was restless, like I shouldn't be there, but I didn't want to be anywhere else.

I took a nap and was awakened by Jane's voice squawking through our walkies giving us her location. You could hear the "oohs" and "ahs" of the passengers as Jane reminded me to put the Moët on ice.

"Tough luck today, mate," someone said. "Full house for the sunset ride." I had my sights aimed at a sunset trip. With the evening flight booked, I would remain part of the chase crew one more day. It didn't do much for my declining mood.

We followed Jane's co-ordinates and soon found the balloon drifting toward us. She brought it down within fifty feet of the van. The passengers flopped out of the basket, and ran to the Champagne like kids to candy, their voices an octave higher than when they took off.

I was happy for them, it was impossible not to be. But there were miles of fabric to roll up again, and by the time we secured the basket to the top of the van, the two bottles were empty.

After the evening flight, we went to a barbecue at a friend's house. After dinner someone played guitar around a fire. He sang songs from his beloved England. One in particular was about the London rain, the Underground, and foggy mornings. Memories splashed across their faces. They loved ballooning but they missed England, yet it was only an hour away by plane. They could go for the day if they wanted. My country was on the other side of the planet. I went inside and called a taxi. I made some excuse that I didn't feel well and went back to the house.

****

The next day they let me sleep in. When I got up there was coffee and croissants in the kitchen. A note said to stay close to the phone. Someone would call if there was a cancellation. So I spent the morning with Marvin. I put him back in his pool ten times, but he kept ending up on my foot. I helped Chef prepare lunch for the crew, while she told stories of cooking her way around the world.

When Jane and the crew arrived they were in hysterics. No sooner had they taken off, when a female passenger giving fair warning leaned over the side and vomited. Repeatedly. That wasn't the worst. They were passing low over a hotel's outdoor terrace filled with people eating breakfast. The woman, terribly embarrassed, apologized after each convulsion. "Whoops, sorry, love! Terribly sorry! Don't look up! My Lord, when will it end?"

The balloon was drifting so slowly no one on the terrace was spared. When the laughter subsided, Jane mentioned her plan for the sunset flight. If the party didn't show up within their allotted thirty minute grace period, I would hop in. All I needed to do was find these people and tie them up and leave them in a field. Not for long, just until after their grace period.

We prepared the van for the evening flight; sandwiches, cheese, fruit, cold cuts, and Champagne. We headed out, hoping that the passengers would somehow not show up. I'm not a cruel person by nature, just a stubbed toe or a small gash to the forehead would suffice. Maybe a curable infection. Just something to slow them down. Fingers were crossed.

The sky already had the makings of a spectacular sunset. As Jane fired up the burners, I kept an eye on my watch. Ten minutes later the balloon expanded and took shape. So far no one had showed up and I wanted to keep it that way.

Jane triple-checked everything, giving the burners a couple of blasts to smooth out the last ripples in the fabric. I held one of the ropes tightly as the basket stood upright, dancing on a blade of grass. Fifteen minutes to go.

Jane hopped in and went over her pre-flight checklist. With ten minutes to go, I heard something in the distance. My heart sank, certain it was the arriving passengers. But it was just some birds rustling in the trees. The balloon tugged. It wanted to fly, and so did I. Jane checked her watch.

"What a pity," Jane said with perfect British melancholy. "A perfect evening and we have a full cancellation. Don't bump your head on the burners, love." I looked around in disbelief. The crew saluted me and tossed their ropes. The balloon started to rise. I only had an instant to react.

"See you on the other end, mate!" one of them yelled.

I dove in head first. When I got to my feet, we were clearing the tree tops. We ascended slowly over the rolling countryside and drifted toward Chateau d'Amboise. As we passed over its enormous roof, we could see lights on inside. People were scurrying about in the upstairs offices. It takes a lot of people to run a chateau.

I'll never forget the sky. Straight up was light blue, quickly fading to indigo. Below were red, purple, and yellow smears like from an artist's brush. I felt sorry for the canceled party missing all this. But just a little. We drifted toward the setting sun, over a rolling carpet of green, dotted with sheep and narrow paths.

And that's when it hit me like a sonic boom. I grabbed the edge of the basket for balance. My eyes watered and ached. I had been shoving it to the back of my mind for so long, but I couldn't keep it there anymore. My time was ending, fast. If I was honest with myself, which I wasn't, I was merely squeezing in one more adventure before the inevitable.

I had been here for a year and it felt like a week. I hadn't given Laurie next month's rent because I was out of money. I had stretched it as far as it could go, but there was no denying it any longer. I tried to inhale but my breath caught in my throat. Jane broke the long silence.

"This is it for you, isn't it?" she asked.

We had covered a lot of ground since our miserable bus ride together. Our nightly talks in the crew house with good food and wine had made us all close, and they knew me better than I cared to admit. I wasn't the first person who had floated over the Loire and pushed away thoughts of leaving.

"Next week we're going to a balloon festival north of Paris. You could crew for me?" giving me an excuse to stay longer. I nodded, knowing I'd be on a plane over the Atlantic by then.

Jane gave the burners a blast and steered us over a vineyard. Carved out of the middle was a small chateau converted into a restaurant. Outdoor lights ringed a dozen tables with white tablecloths. I could see the silverware glistening under candles. Cars were parked haphazardly among the vines.

News of our approach spread like wildfire. Waiters dressed in black and white ran outside spinning their towels. A car pulled up and an elegantly dressed couple got out. They looked up and waved like children. We were so close, I could see her jewelry sparkling around her neck.

The man yelled to us, "Descendez! Un coup de Champagne pour vous!" Yes, Jane, land this thing and he'll buy us a glass of Champagne. But it was asking too much.

"It would be a hell of an entrance, love, but we'd never get her off again. I'm on thin ice as it is." She was right. The people probably arrived within their thirty-minute grace period and were on the phone to Jane's boss right this minute raising bloody hell. But it would be perfect, wouldn't it? Champagne among the vines.

The couple headed inside, but the waiters chased us, towels twirling, through the vines and into an open field. They bent over, hands on knees to catch their breath. Yes, even they had to return to reality. Jane grabbed the walkie and informed the crew where we'd be touching down.

I saw the van kick up dust on the river road. Up ahead was the Loire River. We dipped lower, maybe fifty feet over it. Jane added a quick burst of heat. It takes ten seconds for the balloon to respond. We dipped again. Another blast. Cars had stopped and people were pointing at the beautiful monster floating over their river.

Thirty feet. Another roaring blast. I looked down. Ten feet, with the balloon reflected in the water. Jane cranked both burners full bore. They roared like a jet on takeoff. The heat singed my neck.

Just as the noise became unbearable, she shut the burners down. Not a sound. The basket kissed the water. Barely a ripple as we bobbed along. I heard a peep. Marvin crawled out of Jane's flight bag. Probably heard the water. He crawled onto my shoe, flapping his little wings, wanting to come topside. I picked him up and placed him on the edge of the basket.

He stared into the water. And then he leaped, wings flapping like crazy, but he went straight down. He splashed and rolled upright like a rubber ducky. He swam in tight circles looking up at me, quacking.

Then silently, we lifted off. I reached out for Marvin but he was too far. Jane handed me a stick. I stuck it in the water. Marvin swam to it and hopped on. I placed him back on the edge of the basket. We watched our reflections shrink in the water as we cleared a bridge.

Up ahead I saw the chase van. The crew twirled anything they could find over their heads; towels, jackets, someone waved a leafy tree branch. And there was a new face in the crowd. Chef had come along. She was beautiful even from a hundred feet in the air.

We softly touched down in a field. I hopped out. Jane handed me Marvin. On the white tablecloth there was a spread to die for. Thanks, Chef. We ate and drank with

Marvin on my knee. We watched the sunset together. We told stories and laughed, and I felt like I'd known everyone for years. But when the last rays of the setting sun disappeared, it was over. Marvin and the Moët helped, but it was over.

It's Over

The next day I rode the train back to Paris with Jane and her crew. Marvin and Chef stayed behind, unfortunately. They'd hold the fort down while the rest continued on to the balloon festival north of Paris.

I stepped onto the platform and waved good-bye to everyone. Jane lowered her window and said she wanted to see California, and since she was my favorite hot air balloon pilot, she had an open invitation. I waved until they left the station.

It felt like when I said goodbye to Silvia and Alessandra. I grabbed my bag and headed down the platform. For the first time since I arrived in Paris, I didn't know what to do. Everyone was running to catch their train. The giant board ticked off places I'd seen. I headed for the Métro. I got off several stops early. I needed to walk. I noticed things I hadn't seen before, even though I had walked these streets countless times.

I grabbed a sidewalk table and ordered the biggest beer they had. I watched cars, jaywalkers, and shoppers pass. I looked at the corner where I had ordered a Crêpe

Grarnyeranyeryay. I still can't say it, but I wanted to stay until I could.

Across the street was where I met Laurie for the first time. I watched people enter and exit my boulangerie. How many baguettes did I buy there--a hundred, two hundred? I remembered how patient they were when all I could do was point at what I wanted. I should go and thank them, but I'd probably clam up. Or worse.

Thoughts swirled around me: my dears Framboise, Hélène, and Momma, Augustin's ghost stories, my school, Yoko's death run, Groucho Marx, Ana on Juan's shoulders, Roland and Marie-Hélène who cooked our pasta, chicken sandwiches at dawn, the dog on the alpine roof, Mark in Verona, Bobby and Markus, the brothers of San Remo, spitting goats, camels and turbans, and Marvin. And so much more.

I thought of things I had to do: pack, close my bank account, what was left of it anyway, say goodbye (ugh), and figure out what to do when I returned. I ordered another beer instead.

****

Laurie brought a smarmy college boy by to look at the apartment. He strutted in, hair flopping in his face, full of himself. He smirked at me as he passed. Laurie didn't want to rent to him, but she still didn't want to give the apartment up. It was that kind of place.

She showed him how the water heater and butane tank worked. He thought it trite. He snickered at the small kitchen and scoffed at the too small dining table. This was an eighteen-year old on Daddy's money. He wanted me out so he could hang out with his friends and spend their evening combing their hair.

I watched him in the bathroom. He didn't look out the window and Laurie didn't show him. She shot me a look like, give me the word and I'll tell this punk to shove off. But we both knew that wouldn't happen. The little brat wanted to sign the lease right in front of me. Laurie refused. Tomorrow would be fine.

That night I was angrier than I had ever been in my life. But at who? At what? I felt as though I hadn't seen the Eiffel Tower since I arrived, but I couldn't remember a day I didn't. I hadn't seen enough things; but I was forever visiting churches, museums, quartiers, stores, and monuments.

I didn't spend enough time with my friends, but I was forever with them, Jullouville, Mont Saint-Michel, picnics, movies, cafés. I didn't learn enough about their language, or their wine and food, but I ate and drank all the time. Boy, did I eat and drink all the time.

That one night last fall when I didn't feel well, why didn't I go out anyway? Didn't I know a night at home was a night wasted? I didn't want to go back home, but I couldn't stay. Could I ever come back for a vacation on a packaged tour? Take photos of the Tower from a bus? I love Paris but maybe I'd ruined it. One thing's for sure: the money was gone. It lasted longer than I ever imagined, but it was gone.

The next morning, I put my bags at the door and made a last check of everything. Oddly, I was leaving with less than I came with. No reason to lug home worn-out clothes and half-filled toiletries. I packed my wool coat instead. I don't know why; it was in the worst shape of all. But it held so many memories, I couldn't let it go.

I went into the kitchen. I could hear the chatter of my parties, pots clanging, Ana clomping around. I dug out the wooden spoon and clanged the butane tank. Empty. Perfect. Let floppy hair college boy deal with it.

I went to the bathroom window and looked at the Tower. It was hard to make out in the haze, but it was there, daring me to leave. I imagined Marvin sitting on the ledge, staring down, wondering if he should make the leap. I hoped he was okay while the crew was up north. Chef would take care of him.

A horn honked outside. Laurie, taking me to the airport. Just like her to be on time. I carried my bags to the elevator. I rode it down; with the added weight, it glided down instead of rattling off the sides. At the bottom, I put the bags out, and got back in and pushed the 6th floor button. Up I went, bouncing off the sides. I never realized how a silly sound could mean so much. I stepped onto the landing. I looked at my door to the left, then right, then upstairs to Marie-Hélène and Roland's door, where they cooked our dinner and saved my ass. It was eerily silent.

I got back in and rattled to the bottom. I stepped out, shutting the cage door for the last time. A door slam echoed down the stairwell. The elevator rose and disappeared into the darkness. I heard someone get in and the cage shut. I hustled across the courtyard. I didn't want to talk to anyone.

Laurie was leaning against her car tapping her foot impatiently. She was double-parked on the sidewalk. I tossed my bags in the back and hopped in front.

We got on the Périphérique at Porte de Versailles. There was no need to talk. Laurie knew what was going on in my head. I spent many evenings eating and talking at her place with her many interesting friends. She was probably thinking about the day she might have to give up her place and return to Canada.

I saw the RER roar past. I thought of my first day when I rode it in, counting the stops to Châtelet, sweating in my coat, and popping up at Saint-Michel for my first breath of Paris.

We swung north on the east side of the city. I looked to my right at the suburbs. Laurie whacked my leg. "C'mon, it's your last day." She was right. I looked to the left. The haze had cleared. Paris was radiant, postcard beautiful.

I didn't even mind looking at the horrific Tour Montparnasse. Well, a little.

I saw the Eiffel Tower way across town, then picked out other sites; the blue blob of the Pompidou Center, the Tour Saint-Jacques at Châtelet, the Louvre. Then my stomach turned over. There was one more thing to see as we approached the exit for Charles de Gaulle airport.

At the north end of the city, up on the butte, sat Sacré-Cœur, my landmark welcoming me to the city, seemingly weeks ago, but it had been over a year. This time, it said good-bye. It was so white, and so beautiful, and so perfect, against the blue sky. And then it was gone. And so was I.

I don't remember anything else of the trip to the airport. I had nothing to carry on. I took a seat by the window and watched the ground crew load the luggage. No one sat next to me. It was hard to fathom. I had planned on a year, but I learned quickly where to buy and eat cheaply enough, and it had lasted well over that. Sitting there I thought of the obnoxious guy next to me.

"Then what?"

"More than you'll ever know," I mumbled as I buckled up. I reached in my pocket and pulled out a wine cork. It was from the first bottle I drank when I arrived, a pedestrian Rhône I'd bought at a chain wine shop. It wasn't that good; but with the thrill of being in Paris, I was "aux anges," with the angels, with it. I rolled the cork around between thumb and forefinger, remembering it. Back home I'd look for it, but didn't hold out hope of finding it. But I could try.

We taxied forever through a shroud of grey. We waited forever for our turn to take off. You get to a point where you think, just go already.

I had no plan when I landed. Just like when I arrived. I stared at the back of the seat in front of me as the acceleration pushed me back in mine. And just like that, we tilted back, and left the ground.

When I get home I'll make some calls, see some friends. But after that, I'll rack my brain to figure out how to get back to Paris. And when I do, I'll walk with Dominique along the Seine, and we'll have a good time.

Updates

Framboise and her husband Antoine live in Paris with their three children; Jules, Marie, and Louise (Loulou!).

Hélène and her husband Dario live in Rome with their four daughters; Maylis (named after Momma), Pauline, and twins Sophie and Juliette.

Momma and her husband Jean-Marc live in Paris with their two children; Théophile and Diane.

The bridge Katie and I walked over Lake Lucerne burned down. It's rebuilt, but the priceless etchings are gone forever. I never heard from Katie. I hope she's doing well, and somehow, some way, reads this.

Sadly, Didi and Carola divorced. They live in Ulm and have two beautiful daughters; Julia and Katja.

Katrina is a doctor, probably specializing in foot removal surgery.

Silvia is a Buddhist. In Italy. How does that work?

Mark and his wife Louise (poor thing) live in storybook Cambridgeshire with their two daughters Maisy and Freya.

Markus, no doubt, is watching *Critters* and *Critters 2* on his *Critters: the Ultimate Collection DVD*. Since the release of *Critters 3*, I have not heard a word from him.

I never saw my upstairs neighbors Marie-Hélène and Roland again, but I wish them well. Thank you for the thank-you card. I still have it.

I never saw Lazslo the mad Hungarian again. But word is he's out there somewhere, twirling his socks.

The brothers of San Remo closed their restaurant and retired. In separate towns.

Laurie returned to Toronto and became a film maker.

With Amel holding his hand, Peter could bear the pain no longer, and died of cancer at the age of 38. It was the cause of his sudden outbursts. If she ever reads this, I wish her well.

Papa passed away. *Prost*, Papa!

My rumpled wool coat with the shoe print on the shoulder still hangs in my closet. It looks horrid. I wear it often.

####

About the Author

The author has a lifelong fascination with Europe. This is his first book, stories about dropping everything and moving to Paris. He sleeps in Los Angeles, but dreams of Paris. He travels there often to make sure his friends are raising their children properly, and won't forget their "American uncle."

Email me Kevin@KevinMcDonoughBooks.com
Friend me on Facebook:
https://www.facebook.com/kevinmcdonoughbooks

Please remember to leave a review of my book at your favorite retailer, or at my website:
www.KevinMcDonoughBooks.com

A Sneak Peek of my next book, "Re-entry."

Chapter 1
B-4, Aisle 12

It was strange being back in the States after a long time in Paris. Walking through the airport to Baggage Claim I noticed things that foreigners notice but we Americans are immune to; overweight people. Not the "I'll leave my shirt untucked because it's warm" crowd, but grossly overweight, children and adults alike. They didn't get that way during the time I was gone, this girth was built pound by pound, year after year. Yet, it was shocking to see so many of them wearing clothes hanging like tents.

Sure, I saw overweight people in Europe, but they were rare, and stuck out like sore thumbs. Here they blended in, until you sharpened your focus. The advertisements on the walls made it clear that fast-food restaurants had run out of angles to market their burgers, except to make them bigger. The single patties were gone, and the double-decker was an endangered species. Triple patties led the way, piled sky-high with thick slices of tomato, slabs of cheese, fried onion rings, French fries, bacon, guacamole, jalapeños, their special sauce, and short ribs.

French fries, if the ones stuffed into the burger weren't enough, were served in buckets and offered with all sorts of dipping sauces. Sodas came in wastebasket-sized cups. The food got bigger, and waistlines followed suit.

Outside I was staggered by the size of the SUVs. They had somehow survived every gas price hike and were bigger than ever. I stood next to one at the curb, feeling the heat rise out of the wheel wells from the massive engine, like a fire breathing dragon. The wheels were almost as tall as me. Then it all made grotesque sense. The people eating these monster burgers needed monster vehicles to shuttle them around.

Waiting in line at a supermarket, I stared at a young woman's neck. I don't usually stare; I do it discretely, but she had a snake tattoo crawling out of her collar and up her neck. It wrapped around until the head flicked its forked tongue at her ear lobe. On the top of her foot was the snake's rattle. It coiled around her leg and disappeared into her shorts.

When she stepped forward to pay for her groceries I turned to a smiling woman behind me. "Isn't that gorgeous?" she asked me, admiring the woman's snake, "Just the prettiest thing I've ever seen." She had a cross tattooed on her arm, and appeared ready to ask the snake lady how she could get a five-foot rattler needle stamped on her. "I'm sorry, were you going to say something?" she asked me.

I studied the other people in line and pushing carts up and down the aisles. Most of them had tattoos, many with several. While I was in Paris, some huckster had convinced women that these purple blobs looked good on them. We Americans, it seemed, can be convinced to buy anything; Pet Rocks, Beanie Babies, Chia Pets, and now tattoos. The cashier had one, the young lady who bagged my groceries had several, and a woman dumping her change into a coin machine at the exit had several.

After I settled into an apartment I made some phone calls to let people know I was back and ready to work, or at least remind them who I was. Half the numbers were disconnected, production companies had seemingly dried up and blown away.

When I left for Paris reality television was in its infancy, the bastard child of a few struggling cable channels. When I returned they ruled the airwaves. When I finally got through, I couldn't believe what I was hearing.

"Wait," I said, "the show moves a dozen misfits into a house? Is there a script?...No? How do they know what to do? They don't? What kind of a show is that?" She hung up on me.

I got through to another company, but it was more of the same. "Bratty kids strut their stuff while their obnoxious parents live vicariously through them when "high jinx" ensues? Who would watch that? She hung up on me, too.

The wave of Reality TV slammed into Hollywood, gathered up writers, directors, and producers, and swept them away in the receding tide, never to be heard from again. Well, I thought, it won't last. But like disco and rap before it, Reality TV proved me wrong.

A few friends clung to their jobs for dear life, but they knew it was over, just waiting for the studio to throw them out, to be replaced by something new on the cheap.

I wasn't going to take this lying down, so I signed up with a temp agency, just until this reality stuff blew over. A lady read my application and asked me what type of work I was looking for. I started to give her a rundown of my experience, but she cut me off.

"Hold on, Bucko, we have two categories. Office work, which is filing and phone work. Are you familiar with voice and e-mail, Centrex, Meridian, and other relay-based telecommunications systems?" I felt NO APPLICABLE SKILLS flash across my forehead. "How about light industrial?"

"Light industrial, what?" I asked.

"Warehousing, fork lifting, janitorial." I blinked. "What exactly can you do?" she asked. When I blinked again, she handed me a time slip. "When you finish a job have your employer sign at the bottom. Mail it Friday. You'll be paid within ten days."

"Do you have any idea when I might be called?" I asked, anxious to get to work.

"Demand is slow right now, and we give preference to our regulars, but we'll do what we can." I went home and got back on the phone for one last shot.

"Let me get this straight," I said, squinting to concentrate, "you're going to provide a woman with a life coach, therapist, nutritionist, trainer, cosmetic surgeon, stylist, and dentist, and give her a total transformation so she can find a date? What kind of nut would do that?…Really, thousands?" I hung up on them.

The phone rang at 4:30 the next morning. I whacked the receiver off the hook. Groping in the dark, I reeled it in and heard a woman's perky voice on the other end. "Good morning! We have a job at a warehouse. Are you interested?"

"I've told you people before I only want the Sunday paper," I said, shaking the cobwebs out of my brain.

"Sir, this is the temp agency. We have you on file as available for work. It's one of our best customers. Can you be there by six o'clock?" I squinted at the clock.

"The six o'clock coming up, or the other one?"

"When you get there, ask for J.R." she said, ignoring me.

I scribbled down the address and stumbled into the shower. I wanted to make a good impression so I shaved, put on a pair of khakis, polo shirt, and dress loafers. I wasn't sure what I'd be doing, but I didn't want to be underdressed.

The warehouse was in a bad part of town. I parked in a potholed lot next to a trampled chain link fence that separated it from mountains of junk and debris. I checked the address, hoping I'd made a mistake. I smoothed out my khakis, and entered a small filthy office.

There was a layer of grime on everything, including the guy behind the counter. "Excuse me," I said, trying to sound cheery at six in the morning. "I'm looking for J.R." Grimy Guy looked up from his catalog and eyed me through his smeared eyeglasses with disdain.

"You from the agency?" he asked.

"Yes. Are you J.R.?" I asked, still polite, for me.

"Take a seat and grab a coffee."

"Terrific, but I'm supposed to check in with J.R." I persisted.

"J.R. gets here when he gets here. Now get some coffee and relax." I placed a filthy newspaper on a filthy chair and sat on my hands. I could tell he was studying me from behind his taped up, thick eyeglasses. Too much staring into those catalogs. "Ever worked in a warehouse before?" he asked.

"Me? No," I said, as I checked the crease in my khakis.

He mumbled something and went back to his catalog. I was fidgety because I was programmed to hit the ground running when arriving at work. I could sit for an interview, but when I'm on the clock I want to get going. But orders are orders, so I poured hands down the worst cup of coffee in my life from an old, encrusted pot.

J.R. shuffled in an hour later. I stood up and introduced myself. He eyed me up and down as passed without a word, with the same disdain as Grimy Guy, and rounded the counter behind him.

"Yep, that's what they sent us" Grimy Guy said, answering J.R.'s unasked question. I followed J.R. around the counter and through a door into a massive warehouse. There were endless rows of industrial shelves so long they disappeared into a haze. They were stacked to the heavens with crates of toilets. *So, this is what my life has come to.*

I could barely keep up with J.R. as he headed for the kitchen in the far corner. I tried some small talk, but he refused to communicate with the outside world until after two cups of industrial strength instant coffee. I sat across from him at a small table as he read the paper. J.R. was a lifer and couldn't care less if a lick of work got done. Halfway through his third cup J.R. became, not nice, but civil. "Ever wrapped a palette?" he asked, hoping to find some common ground between us.

"What's a palette?"

He cocked his head, like a dog hearing an odd frequency. "What the toilets sit on," he answered. "Ever wrapped one?"

"As a gift?"

"What rock did they find you under?" he asked.

"I don't know about that," I replied, "but the agency--"

"--Ah, the agency." J.R. didn't like the agency. Over the years they'd sent over too many like me who didn't know a palette from a petunia. And anyone who walked the earth not knowing the difference had no place in his life.

Palettes are the cornerstones of warehouses. The ebb and flow. Nothing gets done without one. No shipping, no receiving, no stocking. And I didn't have a clue what one was. "Can you drive a fork lift?" he asked.

"Driven hundreds of them," I replied, having flunked my palette exam. "I drive them all the time." *In my khakis and loafers.* J.R. refilled his coffee and headed out. I followed him across the polished concrete floor to a row of forklifts lined up against the wall like a showroom. A pair of thick cables snaked out of them and into a massive battery charger on the wall. J.R. handed me a copy of the order sheet.

"Get me a Desert Blue Silent Flush off B-4, aisle twelve." I grabbed the purchase order and dashed off, happy to have something to do. I was half way across the warehouse before I realized I had no idea what he was talking about. "Hey!" he yelled. I slipped to a stop in my leather soles. J.R. jerked his thumb at the forklifts, "aren't you going to take one of these?"

"I'll scout it out first, then come back for it," I lied. There was no way I would climb into one of those monsters with him watching me. "Where'd you say it was again?"

"B-4, aisle twelve."

"Right. A Quiet Blue Dessert Flusher, what?"

"Desert Blue Silent Flush, B-4, aisle twelve." I strutted confidently across the floor as if I knew what I was doing. I scanned the shelves looking for B-4. I darted down an aisle for some privacy. I peeked through a shelf. J.R. was gone, and I knew I wouldn't see him anytime soon.

I cross checked the markings on the aisles with my paperwork. I wandered the endless rows and located aisle twelve. I walked about four miles and found A-1, another four, then A-2. I disappeared into the haze and found B-4. But B-4 went forever with brands like American Standard, Koehler, Glacier Bay, Whitehaus, on and on. Then started the bidets, low-rise, high-rise, with heated water (not a bad idea), and in every color under the sun. My legs ached walking on the concrete, but finally I found the Silent Flushes.

What luck, it was on the bottom shelf, all I had to do was slide it out and push it to the loading dock. I checked the labeling. It was definitely a Silent Flush, but it was Almond, and J.R. wanted Desert Blue. The next shelf up had Beige, the next, Biscuit. Above that was Black, the fifth shelf had Brown, and of course, up in the ozone was Desert Blue. Alphabetical. It was thirty feet up if it was an inch.

I stuffed the order sheet in my back pocket and started climbing. The first two shelves weren't bad, but once I got to the Biscuit level my hands got clammy, and I wasn't even half way there. I wiped them on my khakis and kept going.

I didn't dare look down. I climbed past the Black level, then Brown. I could see the floor below me out the corner of my eye. Then I wondered how heavy one of these crates was, and how would I get it down?

Only about six more feet and I'd be there. I tested each step carefully and pulled even with a crate labeled Desert Blue Silent Flush. Without thinking, I reached in my back pocket for the order sheet, and my foot slipped. I grabbed the shelf above me as my legs bicycled until they found a solid surface. Another brain freeze like that and I'd be a goner.

I grabbed a corner and slid it to the edge. I eased it onto my shoulder. When it tipped over the edge it felt like my knees compressed into my ankles. In a panic, I heaved upwards and slid it back onto the shelf. Perspiration leaped out of me, and my heart was slamming against my chest.

Then I heard a hum. Soft and low at first, then it got louder. Then I heard a different hum, high and whirring. Tongs of a forklift rose past me, scooped up the palette and lowered the Desert Blue Silent Flush to the floor. More whirring, and the tongs appeared again, facing me. They inched closer, as if beckoning me to grab hold. I reached out and hugged a tong. When I was sure I could hold on, I stepped away.

The fork lowered me past the Brown shelf, then Black, then Biscuit. I hoped the ground would open up and I would pass right by Almond and be dropped in the earth. From there I could dig to the parking lot and drive off never to be seen again. But, it slowed and placed me on the Almond level, terra firma.

Orchestrating the rescue mission was a wiry kid who looked much older than he probably was. He maneuvered the levers with one left hand while drinking coffee from the other. He was so thin if he turned sideways he almost disappeared. He tipped his cap and breezed away on his forklift.

I needed to rest, maybe take lunch, but it was only 7:00am. I pushed the crate as hard as I could. The palette slid a foot and stopped, but the toilet kept going and clunked on the concrete floor. I couldn't get it back on the palette, so I pushed it a foot at a time down the aisle.

When I got to the end, the skinny kid circled behind me, and with incredible skill, slid the fork under the toilet crate and placed it onto the palette.

He motioned for me to hop on. We glided across the wide expanse of the warehouse and pulled up to a row of palettes tightly wrapped in plastic, like Christmas presents. That was what J.R. wanted to know, if I knew how to wrap them. He placed the palette in line with the others. I hopped off.

"Name's Gary. Scary Gary, they call me." He smiled and I knew why. He had three, maybe four teeth in his head, and those were teetering on the edge. At lunch I learned why.

Scary Gary ate a simple diet of coffee and sugar. He would fill his coffee mug half-full with sugar, then pour in coffee. He would stir it into a sludge and drink it. Endlessly. He easily consumed a half pound of sugar a day. He was never without that mug, and I never saw him eat or drink anything else. He even topped off his mug before heading to the parking lot at the end of the day. But he was nice to me and helped any way he could.

He was probably a lifer like J.R., but unlike J.R., Gary read incessantly, huge novels, on his breaks, at lunch, even strapped in to his forklift. He was never without his book. Or coffee. But Gary had other things to do besides rescue me atop warehouse shelves. After lunch I was determined to figure this job out on my own.

J.R. appeared out of nowhere with another order form. "Did you pull down the Desert Blue Silent Flush yet?"

"Yep," I said, leaving out Gary's rescue.

"Did you wrap it?"

"...Nope."

"Wrap it, then grab me a Sandstone Dual-Port Circle Swirl, J-2, aisle seventeen. Get 'em wrapped and ready by four o'clock. They gotta be in Tulare by morning." I looked down at the form, and when I looked up he was gone.

Gary pulled a huge roll of plastic wrap off a shelf. He knotted the end under the palette, stuck his fingers in the ends of the roll and, starting from the bottom, circled the palette, letting the plastic unspool, like letting out kite string. As he rose, the toilet disappeared behind a frosty film, so perfect it looked shrink wrapped.

Like a spider, Gary spun a cocoon, anchoring the toilette for transport. He knotted it off at the top and replaced the roll on the shelf. He hopped into his forklift and zoomed away in search of another toilet. *Sheesh, how hard can that be?*

I grabbed the roll and was shocked how heavy it was. Gary might be scary, but he was strong. Knotting off the end wasn't too difficult, but holding the roll bent over proved a challenge for me. I hoisted it up high and figured I would start from the top and work down. Same difference, I thought.

When I lifted it over my head I knew I wouldn't be able to hold it there long, so I ran around the palette. In a few seconds my hands were burning like fire. I dropped the roll and it unrolled across the warehouse floor. My hands were shredded. Spinning the roll caused friction, and now my hands were bleeding. Gary had calluses, I didn't.

I ran to the kitchen for the first aid kit. J.R. looked up from his newspaper and said, "Have to toughen up those hands, kid." *Kid.* I rinsed the blood in the sink and wrapped my hands in paper towels. "Don't use too many," J.R. said, "we use them for toilette paper."

Then the blisters began. Huge heat blisters. I found some ointment in the first aid kit and smeared it on. I taped fresh gauze around both hands and headed back into the warehouse.

There was no way I could hold the plastic roll, so I found a pipe in the equipment room. I rolled up the plastic that got away. What a mess, crinkled and stuck together. I slid the pipe through the roll but I couldn't get any tension on it for a tight fit around the palette. I could make one turn before I had to stop, my hands burning and arms aching from the weight.

The plastic was crinkled before it went on, and by the time I'd finished I could have entered it in a post-modern sculpture competition. Up until then I'd seen no one else but Gary and J.R. in the warehouse, but now they were coming out of the woodwork to look at my creation. Workers circled the crumpled mess, taking pictures on their phones for proof of what they saw.

Then a big rig backed up to the loading dock. The driver got out and joined the crowd. He circled my work, then eyed everyone, stopping on me. "I cain't load dat thang! You wrapped this? Where'd they find you?"

Before he added more insults, Gary screeched his forklift to a stop, making him hop back. Gary ripped off the crinkled wrap. In no time he spun a new cocoon around my Desert Blue Silent Flush, from B-4, aisle twelve. J.R.

asked me about the Sandstone Dual-Port Circle Swirl. I told him it was coming right up and headed out to find it.

I found the Dual-Port Circle Swirl, but being Sandstone, it was alphabetically at the top like Desert Blue Silent Flush. I wasn't about to climb up again. What I needed was a forklift with training wheels, and I almost found it.

It was off by itself, away from the monster forklifts sucking up electricity from the massive wall charger. It was a palette jack, a walking forklift. I had seen one of the workers using one earlier. Designed to only move a palette from Point A to B, not reach fifty feet for it, you walked behind it and steered it with a handle and twist throttle. It was the low-rider of forklifts.

Backed against the wall, it was aimed toward the middle of the warehouse. Perfect, at least I wouldn't have to maneuver it right off the bat. I flipped the power switch. An amber light glowed above it. I twisted the throttle and it inched backward. It worked the opposite of a motorcycle, twisting under was reverse. I twisted over and it inched forward. I walked it about ten feet until I was in the clear, and then aimed it across the warehouse.

I had lots of room so I thought I'd practice a little before heading down aisle twelve for the Dual-Port Circle Swirl. I turned left, not knowing it steered by the rear wheels, and that's when it got away from me.

It picked up speed as it headed right for the boss's office. Out of nowhere, Gary glided past and saw it. Like a tugboat guiding the QE2, he approached alongside and nudged towards the loading dock. He peeled off at the last second, never spilling a drop of his coffee.

The palette jack zoomed past the wrapped palettes and launched itself off the loading dock. It sailed through the air and landed, forks down, into a metal dumpster. It rattled like thunder, its rear wheels still spinning in the air.

Gary pulled up on his forklift. I'm pretty sure it was the first time for Gary and me to see a palette jack sticking out of a dumpster. He patted me on the back and explained, after a long gulp, it had a faulty kill switch. That was why it was over by itself.

Oh.

After my shift I went to the temp agency. I sat there, hands wrapped in gauze. "You did *what?*" my temp agent asked.

"I turned left, but it went right."

"That's because it steers by the rear wheels, even I know that. Where is it?"

"It's, uh, where I left it."

"Which is where?" I told her. "You could have killed someone." She called the warehouse and took some heat. They were willing to let me come back if I promised not to touch any machinery. I agreed.

On the way home I bought some ointment and gauze at a pharmacy. When I got home I sat on the sofa and stared at the wall sipping a beer, dreading going back tomorrow. I leafed through a list of phone numbers. There was one left. I dialed. I listened for a few moments to possibly the worst show idea I'd ever heard, then hung up.

I made dinner, changed the gauze on my hands, and set the alarm for five o'clock. I crawled into bed and closed my eyes. I saw the view from the top of Samaritaine, I heard Augustin's hilarious ghost story, and I saw Dominique's pretty face. I drifted off to sleep with those thoughts, and many more, dancing in my head. But mostly I thought of Dominique.

Chapter 2
The Blue Flash

Driving in the next day I was thinking about the Sandstone Dual-Port Circle Swirl. It was supposed to go out with the Desert Blue Silent Flush to Tulare. When I pulled into the parking lot I could see the palette jack's rear wheels still sticking out the top. Gary was on his tiptoes scratching his head staring into the dumpster. I slinked down in my seat and watched Gary mount his forklift and manipulate the tongs like a brain surgeon.

He got the fork under the dumpster and tipped it on its side. Then it was just a matter of slipping the fork under the jack's rear wheels and lifting it out. He backed up and placed it on the loading dock. Then he gulped down the rest of his coffee and sped up the ramp ready for a day's work.

Gary and I forged an unusual friendship. At lunch we talked about books he'd read and about my former profession. He asked if I'd worked with a certain actress. I had, and he proceeded to tell me what he'd like to do to her, bent over his favorite forklift, Lulabelle. Scary Gary, indeed. After that, I made it a point to only talk about books.

Gary decided it was time for me to learn to drive a forklift. He went to our white-haired boss, whose office I almost demolished the day before, and explained he'd take me under his wing.

"It's your life," he told Gary. "Hey," he called to me, "how did you get warehouse work?"

"I checked the box on the app for light industrial," I told him.

"Uncheck it," he advised, and slammed his office door.

It didn't look that difficult, there were half a dozen forklifts buzzing around throughout the day. These guys talked on their phones, read the sports section, any number of things while they zipped around.

I hopped into a shiny yellow one. Gary attached my safety harness. Check. It worked much like the palette jack, except when your turned right, the damn thing turned right. Gary told me to look over the instruction panels while he went for a coffee refill. The instructions were straightforward, push the yellow lever to go forward, pull it for reverse. Accelerator on the right, brake on the left. Double check.

I felt pretty good up there in the cage like the big boys. I twisted the throttle but nothing happened. I studied the instruction panels. There was a safety pedal release. I stepped on it not realizing I had the throttle open. I never knew fork lifts could burn rubber.

It took off like a rocket, then screeched to a stop when my foot slipped of the safety release, slamming me against the cage. Not a good start. I tried again. The motor hummed but I wasn't moving. I added a little more juice. I could feel she was itching to go but couldn't. That's when I heard a cracking sound.

I turned around. I was still hooked up to the charger. The cables were stretched tight and I was slowly pulling the enormous charger out of the wall. I pulled the yellow lever back. The forklift screeched backwards over the cables, tangling around the rear wheels. It was a mess, and I did it all by myself.

Gary hadn't disconnected the cables. In fairness, he didn't know I was going for an unplanned joy ride. I hopped out and studied the twisted mess. I yanked the cables but couldn't budge them. I gave it one more try. A blue arc shot knocked me back against the Coke machine. I slumped down, out cold, and woke up wedged under a shelf. Gary dragged me out by my ankles.

Rather than being upset, Gary accepted me into the Mega Watt Club; a forklift version of the Mile High Club, where acceptance requires a heart-stopping jolt of electricity and singed hair.

Gary nursed a gulp of his coffee sludge down my throat. It wired me worse than the megavolts. He untangled the mess as easily as he had flipped a palette jack out of a dumpster. He drove it out to the center of the warehouse, placed a few orange cones around and told me to get behind the controls.

I wasn't too keen on climbing back in the saddle, but I didn't have the rent for next month and was determined to stick it out. I climbed in and attached the safety harness. "Just think of her as a sexy woman," Gary said.

Uh oh...

He made an off-color reference to the actress he spoke of earlier, and I realized he was hoping I might introduce him to her. I worked with her once. I had no more access to her than Gary did, but he'd never understand that. He talked me through the instruction panels on proper procedure and safety.

I looked over my shoulder to make sure the coast was clear, like I was merging onto the interstate. I stepped on the release pedal and gently pressed the accelerator. The fork lift lurched softly, then purred like a kitten across the smooth concrete floor.

There was plenty of room, mostly because the other forklifts swerved wide around me. Nearing the far end, I made a wide turn and returned to the orange cones. Gary encouraged me all the way. I stopped, then pulled away again, heading down the other end of the warehouse.

By the time I turned around I felt pretty good about myself, which is the worst thing you can do while learning to drive a forklift. I weaved left, then right, then carved a big circle, unaware I was gaining speed. They should put speedometers on those things.

I was enjoying the wind in my hair when I got an impulse for a figure eight. I busted off a left, then a right, and finished up with a figure eight. The adrenaline rush was fantastic. That's when Gary yelled something.

"What?" I shouted as I flew past. Up ahead the white haired boss came out of his office reading some reports. He froze when he saw me barreling down on him. He darted right. I swung left into the cables. I lost control and rammed into the wall. I was so busy pulling and pushing levers I forgot I was standing on the accelerator. The forklift bucked against the wall.

Gary reached in and hit the kill switch. I jumped down and assessed the damage to the wall. I looked at the chewed up cables still snaked across the floor, then at the white haired boss. Then I looked at Gary, grinning from ear to ear. And in that nearly toothless mouth I saw my future. Premature back aches, rescuing novice warehouse workers from forklifts, and annually losing a few teeth until there were none left.

The white haired boss came over. We had a brief chat and it was decided I would get in my car right now and never return. I'd get paid for the day, just leave. Gary stood up for me, but the white haired boss cut him off. I thanked Gary for all he had done. We shook hands. I walked past the Desert Blue Silent Flush, still waiting for its Sandstone Dual Port Circle Swirl partner to be shipped to Tulare. I walked down the loading dock steps past the dumpster, and got in my car and slammed the door. *Wasn't I floating across the Loire in a balloon with Marvin last week?*

I knew moving to Paris would present challenges, but I never dreamed coming back to my country I would feel so alien, so lost. As much as we try to fool ourselves that we're endlessly adaptable, eventually the truth comes crashing down on us. I had no more business driving that forklift than the man in the moon.

I drove straight home. There was no point stopping by the temp agency. They'd get the gory details soon enough. And when they did, that would be the end of my temp work.

Or so I thought.

Made in the USA
San Bernardino, CA
03 June 2018